EVANGELIZATION
in the
AMERICAN CONTEXT

EVANGELIZATION
in the
AMERICAN CONTEXT

David B. Burrell, C.S.C.
and Franzita Kane, C.S.C.
editors

UNIVERSITY OF NOTRE DAME

Library of Congress Cataloging in Publication Data

Main entry under title:

Evangelization in the American context.

   Proceedings of a symposium held at the University of Notre Dame, Jan. 11–13, 1976.
   1. Pastoral theology—Catholic Church—
Congresses. 2. Catholic Church in the United
States—Congresses. 3. Catholic learning and
scholarship—Congresses. I. Burrell, David B.
II. Kane, Franzita, 1909–   III. Notre Dame,
Ind. University.
BX1913.E9   269′.2   76-22403
ISBN 0-268-00901-5
ISBN 0-268-00902-3 pbk.

Manufactured in the United States of America

Contents

Preface

One hundred and ten participants—members of the hierarchy, Catholic college and university administrators, and scholars—gathered at the University of Notre Dame, January 11-13, 1976, at the invitation of the Reverend Theodore M. Hesburgh, C.S.C., president, for a symposium on "Evangelization in the American Context: The Pastoral Presence in an Open Society," under the direction of the Reverend David Burrell, C.S.C., Chairman of the Department of Theology of Notre Dame.

The genesis of the present publication is in a real sense the same as that of the symposium itself. Reflection on "Vatican Council: Ten Years Later," linked to the International Federation of Catholic Universities (IFCU) of Salamanca, 1973, provided Father Hesburgh with the matrix in which his initial projection of the meeting came within the nurturing care of all who began to give it vitality, most especially from January 1975. Its timeliness was voiced unqualifiedly by Bishop James S. Rausch at Catholic University in March 1974: "The relationship between bishops and scholars in the Church is the single most important issue which requires attention in our time.... There exists an urgent need for us to sit down and work out our relationship and discover our mutual need for one another."

From Father Burrell's initial announcement, in July 1975, that Father Hesburgh with the support of Archbishop William D. Borders proposed such a convocation, collaboration in the work took new shape as concrete proposals and enthusiastic response came from across the country. From that general affirmation, and in sessions modeling the interaction which later proved to be the dynamic center of the symposium itself, the twenty members of the Planning Committee, meeting in September 1975, opened up a wellspring of ideas. Although their names are listed here, the debt is beyond any simple acknowledgement. That group honed the generalizations of "evangelization" and "pastoral" to the basic concepts of relationships between Catholic higher education in research, teaching, service, and bishops as pastors and teachers, serving. They settled on six areas for discussion groups—the local Church vis-à-vis neighborhood and society; Catholic identity; prayer and spiritual formation; new forms of ministry; economic concerns; and public policy questions—and provided the discussion leaders who subsequently guided the three days of mutual appraisal and reappraisal. They also provided me with counselors through the fall and winter, especially in the spiritual wisdom of Monsignor John Egan and the practical wisdom of Monsignor John Murphy.

From that September planning session, too, came what Bishop Dozier in January was to call the cutting edge we must restore: "In all decisions the cutting edge must be the gospel; we are habituated to separate moral decisions and political or social." The "cutting edge" we needed, in the aspect of "pray together" and "gathered in my name" came via Bishop Law's insistence that our gathering must pray fervently together as well as think and talk together, and Bishop Szoka's urging of provision of time and space for *being* together. With that rootedness, the meeting properly earned its title of *symposium*.

What I have suggested is sufficient to underscore the collaborative effort which makes the *Proceedings* cover far longer time than the precious days of January 1976, and an extent far greater than the recorded materials gathered here, valuable as those are, both in themselves and in their seminal instrumentality.

In no way can one claim that the present publication is complete, or that it does justice to the complex of ideas exchanged, by day and by night, among those who came and those who joined us in spirit (like Dr. Frank Broderick who sat all day in airports trying to reach Notre Dame, or like Cardinal Garrone and Bishop Jean Jadot, the Apostolic Delegate, whose commitments kept them from attendance but who sent messages of deep interest and encouragement); or those who, out of large and generous habit put into writing of their own accord reflections sent to the press or to us (such as Joseph Cunneen, who flew from our meeting directly to Cuernavaca for an IDOC seminar, thus evidencing his right to urge us now to "broaden our horizons"; the excerpts from his reflective letter to me belong by right in this publication, and may stand for all the other postsymposium analyses one would like to share). Included here, much too briefly, are comments of the Reverend Hervé Carrier, S.J., Rector of the Gregorian University, who came from Rome to represent the International Federation of Catholic Universities of which he is president, and who brought his personal acumen as well as his Gallic wit to enrich the explorations.

I should like to take this opportunity to acknowledge the debt we all have—for me, personally, a joyful one—to the four writers of the background papers, all individuals carrying for the Church heavy obligations: Reverend Donald Merrifield, S.J., Michael Novak, Bishops John S. Cummins and James S. Rausch. Their combined voices separated wheat from chaff for us over the fall and winter.

Some special words of gratitude are indicated elsewhere in the publication, especially to the generous donors who made the symposium possible. And James Langford, director of the Notre Dame University Press, has given invaluable help in connection with all the preparation of the *Proceedings* and its actual publication. To single out any by name is to neglect many; at every turn, the advice, assistance, and professional experience of individuals at Notre Dame were put at my disposal, from James Murphy, Assistant Vice President for Development, to Peggy Roach, Director of the Catholic Committee on Urban Ministry; and very especially, Father Richard Rutherford, C.S.C., liturgist, who gave full reality to our liturgical celebrations.

Beyond all, I have endless obligations to Father Hesburgh, who among his other sustaining support for the preparatory work, generously authorized my attendance with Father Burrell at the organizing meeting of the Inter-University Committee on Research and Policy Studies, called in May 1975 by Dr. Clarence Walton, president of Catholic University. Father Hesburgh's trust and belief made it impossible that the symposium should not exceed its proposed goals.

Such a brief summary may serve to point up what I would like to reaffirm as the great witness given by the symposium in its inception, preparation, and actual experience—what the publisher John H. Finley, Jr. has called "the mystery of collaboration," which he considers even stranger than the mystery of excellence: "In achieving something excellent, a man is with his own thoughts, wresting shape out of half-disorder. . . . in collaboration, two [or, as with us, many] minds cross, each initially private and asking generosity if they are to come together." And he concludes, "The result, when successful, is moving and curiously reassuring; it suggests the difference between Odysseus and the Ancient Mariner, the difference between getting back and not quite getting back from private voyages."

While Father David Burrell was during many months of the year actually *en voyage*, to him I owe the unique privilege I have had to share in some small way in that "mystery of collaboration." Because he was its director, the symposium stands as evidence that none of us were embarked on "a voyage" from which we wanted simply to "get back." Because Father Burrell is, like Robert Lax's Rastelli, "good at talking/ At coffee/ . . . good at juggling on the high wire" (metaphorically speaking, of course), the symposium was far less an Odyssean voyage and far more a Dantean shared pilgrimage into new beginnings.

So it was Bishop Rausch who, on the final evening, after pledging as General Secretary of the USCC, to do all he could in any way in the future to work for the hopes here generated, said that for himself personally the symposium was "the beginning of the unfolding of the dream." For the actualities that these *Proceedings* explore and expand, great gratitude is due; for all that renews our faith and trust that dreams have beginnings in reality—this publication provides a rich range of generating ideas, a challenge to make some radical choices, and the place of the sacred encounter between history and hope.

Sister Franzita Kane, C.S.C.
Notre Dame, Indiana
February 20, 1976

Acknowledgments

Special thanks to Reverend Richard Rutherford, C.S.C., Coordinator of Liturgical Services; to Professor Sue Seid, Director of the University Chapel Choir, and to its 60 student members; to Mr. Scott Dutton, C.S.C., and the Seminarians' Schola.

This symposium has been supported by generous grants from
    Lilly Endowment, Incorporated
    The Raskob Foundation for Catholic Activities, Inc.
    De Rance, Incorporated
    John R. Kennedy Foundation
    An anonymous benefactor

I. OPENING SESSION
January 11

Introduction
David B. Burrell, C.S.C.

I sense an enthusiasm, guarded but genuine, regarding this gathering—and that from people who cannot afford just one more meeting—Father Hervé Carrier from Rome, Monsignor Jack Murphy from Florida (not without complaint, but willingly). It was at Salamanca in 1973 that we sensed it: time to overcome the multiple and regional standoffs between Catholic education and hierarchy. How? By those responsible meeting one another—appreciating each other's concerns: how they diverge, where they intersect. To what end? To learn how much we need each other: pastors, the perspective that research and continuing education can supply; educators, the impetus to encourage the specialized disciplines to focus on some of the pressing human concerns to which bishops must respond for the sake of their people.

It was a difficult symposium to initiate. In academe we can compose conferences over lunch; I know bishops can call one another for the advice they may need. But how to create pathways outside the settled grooves? How to develop avenues of communication where few exist?

For the differing *interests* of educators and pastors—and their specific mandates—will sometimes bring them into conflict. We know that and must respect that fact, for it reflects a fidelity to their respective vocations. Yet there remain two ways through that potential conflict zone: (1) respect for one another—as people we have come to know; (2) appreciation that a pastor as teacher must be informed; and a teacher, as *educator*, shares in a pastoral care.

So we met—a small group composed of pastors and educators—after more than a year of opening consultations with United States Catholic Conference, vacillation (mostly mine), and the delays that accompany a search for funding. It was the conference on research called by Dr. Clarence Walton of Catholic University in May of last year, plus Sister Franzita Kane's promise of organizational assistance, that put us on the track that led to the planning meeting in September.

It was that group which planned these days, as an opportunity for our continuing education, and set them up so that we can learn from one another. We asked a few to be speakers, four persons to provide background for our discussions—Bishops Cummins and Rausch; Father Don Merrifield and Michael Novak—but the primary task of these days lies with the groups.

It is our hope that the discussion groups will (1) identify and illuminate issues, and (2) sketch ways of collaborating to gain insight into those same issues. We are confident that persons who have agreed to speak *to* us will strike many chords of recognition and help to create shared background. But the task of illuminating issues and suggesting concrete ways of interaction to meet them lies with the groups. By the closing session Tuesday evening, we should be able to propose a sufficient number of examples of collaboration to spur imaginations and offer an institutional means for coordinating initial projects.

Remarks

George N. Shuster

Doubtless I have been asked with an affection and esteem I do not merit to chair this meeting because I have seen more of the developing history of religion in the United States than anybody else who could easily be recruited.

I was invited by Monsignor Egan and Father Burrell, and so I should like to begin with a word about each of them, because it will give you some idea of what they thought I would say, though they will probably be disappointed. They organized this conference, very likely the most important in the history of the contemporary Church.

I did not know John Egan personally until a relatively short time ago, but I was aware that he had been for a number of years the priest who cared most about race relations and similar matters.

I was in New York having a quite combative time of my own and had it not been for Cardinal Spellman, who had become a truly good friend, I might well have lost the battle. But anyway, I soon found myself on Saul Alinsky's Board, and even chairman of that organization. I knew little then about Saul's current activities, except that he had entered into some kind of close relationship with the Catholic Archdiocese of Chicago, and that he seemed to be developing his other programs in liaison with Catholic, Protestant, and Jewish groups. I probably helped to undermine the budget of New York City writing letters insisting that John Egan and Saul were not members of the Communist Party. Later on, Cardinal Meyer, perhaps the best friend I have ever had among the hierarchy, received a letter of accusation and did not like it. There is much more to be said, but I do not have the time. But I would like to add that I was the first to ask John Egan to come down here to speak, and that I suggested to Father Hesburgh to establish a pastoral theology program.

I first came to know Father Burrell when we both arrived here about the same time. I was then President Emeritus of Hunter College, and he was a young priest who had been ordained after graduating from Notre Dame, duly membershipped in the Congregation of Holy Cross, and earning his doctorate with distinction. It was always a genuine pleasure for an older man to observe the character and progress of so gifted a younger one.

Now for the substance of my brief story. There have been two highly important periods in the development of educational and cultural relationships between American Catholics and their environment. Ther first was, of course, immigration and linguistic diversity. This, in Europe, had been the basis of the Reformation and the great Romantic Movement, good and evil though it must be in our eyes.

The second was secularization, which began in earnest in the United States after the middle of the nineteenth century, changing the character of many Anglican and Protestant universities. Catholic ones were seriously isolated. But quite apart from academic life, immigration created bitter confrontations, even sometimes bloody ones.

But by and large, the various faiths learned to work together at threshing, barn building, and other pursuits. In Wisconsin, we had our German schools and defended them, not only against John Ireland, but, together with the Lutherans, against the Nativists. But it was in essence a lost cause. There were always some Germans who disliked the Irish. But intermarriage soon put a stop to that. The Irish girls were just too pretty and the German boys too enterprising.

Nevertheless, racial differences still persist and have to be resolved. The rural parishes of some states, for example, have never been reconciled to the new liturgy, and as a result their dedication to parochial schools is far less than it used to be.

Anybody who has lived through this period will have many a chuckle, of course. Thus I can remember well a moment in our local history when a sick pastor in a small Wisconsin town had to request the Brother, who was his jack-of-all-trades, to take his place on Ash Wednesday. But he could not remember the *Memento Homo*, and finally the pastor said in a mood of exasperation—in German of course—"You are a fool and always will be one," the formula the Brother then wrote in ashes on every forehead. It was not too unrealistic, and many probably did not really like it.

The Civil War made great inroads into anti-Catholic Prejudice. The three great poets of the South included two other Catholic priests, and Father John Bannister Tabb was probably the greatest of the three.

But Catholics of the Middle West—by which I mean the territory which extends from New Orleans to Duluth and from Cincinnati to Denver—will not again be dominated by the Eastern cities, either in terms of history or pastoral care. The university simply must pick up the burden of history as well as that of contemporary reality.

The best Catholic architecture, St. Paul's Cathedral and St. John's University, for example, is in the Middle West. And so I think are the best seminaries. But we have had no good biographies of Keane or Katzer, and no studies of pastoral theology, in spite of all the good work that has been done. I am not disparaging the Eastern cities. I lived and worked in one of them for more than thirty years. But they can no longer have a monopoly.

Secularization has doubtless been our principal problem. It began to exert influence in the United States during the middle of the nineteenth century, which soon changed the character of Anglican and Protestant universities and greatly altered the character of those which were Catholic. The Catholic institutions began to suffer greatly from the results of the Modernist controversy. Libraries were depleted of many of their holdings. Even today, there are in some seminaries no copies of Newman's books. Not that Kant and Hegel were probably so bad after all. Romano Guardini was for a time nursed along by Hegel, and Pierre Teilhard de Chardin was, of course.

But over here I give the highest rank to Father Sorin of Notre Dame. When the bishops of the East were at last able to chuckle over the silence of Orestes Brownson, Sorin bravely buried his body in the crypt of Notre Dame's Sacred Heart church. I hope that you will go down there and walk over his body. But Sorin did more. In times of frustration and immense difficulty, he placed over the new university structure he had built a facsimile of the dome of Paris' Hôtel des Invalides, but with a glorious golden figure of Mary on the top. This coincided pretty well with the publication of Adams' *Mont-Saint-Michel and Chartres*. Many now think that the "Golden Dome" is rather sentimental. They are not convinced that a little Jewish girl with a rather dubious biblical history is entitled to a position like this. But the great Breton priest had his day, and he made Notre Dame as surely as Victor Hugo wrote *Les Misérables*.

No university can have all these blessings without being loved, and the Catholic affection for this place has, to a great extent, made the survival of the educated American Catholic's faith in his Church and its institutions possible.

Nor will I ever deny that I have been and still am a Notre Dame football fan, but still how could I ever conceal my admiration for the Jesuits? For the truth of the matter is, that almost every step in my career, insofar as it has been religious, has been taken hand in hand with revered members of the Society both here and abroad. The souls of great men like Gustav Grundlach, Peter Lippert, John LaFarge, and John Murray rest in peace, but if the Church in the United States ever forgets them, it will be a poorer Church. I do not know the Jesuit universities well enough, but I have urged my friend, Father Robert Hartnett, to write a study of them.

In the United States, we face grave problems. The continuing allegiance of the Supreme Court to a purely secularistic interpretation of the Constitution is a very serious handicap. It can be surmounted only by reason, and not by riots. Our theology is, it seems to me, much better despite opposition from Protestant Fundamentalists and Catholic Pentacostals. And I remain quite optimistic about the future provided that what this conference seeks to accomplish—namely, a close liaison between the bishops and educators—can be achieved. The Supreme Court as it has been constituted has been the quintessence of secularism, but it is not a group of evil men. Mr. Justice Douglas is far from being an evil man.

What we must establish is an excellent School of Education. By this I do not mean merely a school which is concerned with pedagogical training for elementary schools and high schools, good though that is, but with pastoral theology, liturgy, journalism, and social action. For a good many years, I thought that Notre Dame and Saint Mary's acting together could provide the basis for such a school. But this is no longer anything I can propose or work toward. It needs a tremendous push from all of you here, and of course, it requires money. But the need is so obvious that a man would have to be blinder than I am not to see it.

The final part of my mission here is to introduce Father Hesburgh. This is a most ridiculous task, since he is by far the best known and most deeply appreciated university president in the United States. But as I have come to realize full well during the fifteen years I have been around here, he is a very great priest who should long since have been a bishop and a cardinal, by reason of his vision of the total mission of the Church.

Whatever Father Hesburgh says over the celestial telephone when I reach heaven will, I am sure, get me in. But that is no special compliment to me. He would have gotten Chou En-lai in too, if he had been asked to do so.

With that, I stop and the symposium begins with Father Hesburgh.

Welcome
Theodore M. Hesburgh, C.S.C.

My first task tonight even before welcoming you is to thank Father David Burrell and Sister Franzita and all of those who have collaborated and supported this conference. I welcome you with a full heart because, while we have 400 conferences in this building every year, this conference is historic and inspiring. It represents a first effort that I hope someday we'll look back on and say, "That night we began. A great good came from it, and we were a part of it." I go to many conferences, as do all of you; many of them I wish I didn't have to go to, but this one I think is going to be most important and I thank each one of you for being here to testify to that importance and to contribute to it.

We should begin tonight by reading you a letter from Cardinal Garrone who is the prefect of the Sacred Congregation for Christian Education:

> Dear Father Hesburgh:
>
> Thank you very much for your kind and gracious letter of the 24th of last month informing me about the projected Symposium to be held at your University from January 11th through the 14th, on the theme "Evangelization in the American Context: The Pastoral Presence in an Open Society." You were so kind as to include a copy of the program and to invite me to attend. However, much as I regret it, I must decline your courteous and gracious invitation because I have previously received an invitation from the Bishop's Conference of Peru to take part in the 12th Inter-American Congress on Catholic Education organized by the Inter-American Federation of Catholic Education. This is to take place in Lima on the exact days, January 11th and following, of your Symposium. My regrets are the keener since, as I note in the letter, the theme of your Symposium is very

near to my concern and dear to my interests. I certainly bless and encourage this undertaking and assure you and your collaborators of my prayers and my great interest. I should like to ask of you the favor of sending me a report of what transpires as well as greeting, in my name, the participants, especially the bishops who will be present. All that can be done to assist bishops to assume their rightful places and duties in the University world as well as to encourage an integration of Catholic colleges and universities into the overall ministry and mission and apostolate of the Church is deeply appreciated.

The task I have is to give a *tour d'horizon*: a look at why we are here, how we came to be here tonight. By way of background, in 1963, the International Federation of Catholic Universities decided to become a more vital force rather than the moribund organization it then was. We took on several new projects. We completely reorganized, we established a Secretariate in Paris, we obtained consultative status with UNESCO; and we created a variety of other things, such as an ecumenical institute in Jerusalem. One of the first tasks that we set ourselves— like everyone else in the 60's—was to try to find out what we were about: what is the nature and function of the Catholic university? We are part of a total spectrum of higher education, in which there are public and private institutions. Protestant, Catholic, and Jewish institutions, private nonsectarian institutions and just about everything else, including proprietary institutions. And we said, "Where do we fit in this spectrum? What is our task, what should we do?"

We began by some meetings at Land-O-Lakes, Wisconsin, a Notre Dame retreat facility. And we had two meetings there, followed by a general conference in Tokyo and one in Kinshasha, where we prepared a document to be discussed. Cardinal Garrone came to Kinshasha and was part of that discussion. Following that, he decided to call many of us to Rome. People were elected from all of the various regions of the world and convened in Rome three years ago in November. There we formulated a document whose themes we had been discussing for almost ten years. After much contention pro and con, we finally elaborated a document on which we all agreed. It proved to be, of course, an on-the-one-hand and on-the-other-hand type of document, since we had people who were concerned about the legitimate requirements of the magisterium with others who were concerned about the legitimate autonomy of universities. No one has an easy answer to this trouble-some problem, yet I think the answer lies in a Spanish proverb, "We find the way by walking." I suspect that this is what we're doing in this meeting.

In any event, after much discussion and negotiation, a document was elaborated. This document has been distributed to all the Catholic universities of the world, and we are trying to live by it. Subsequently, Archbishop Borders and some of his associates set up a committee including university presidents and bishops. They were assisted in this endeavor by Monsignor John F. Murphy, current Executive Director of the College and University Department of the National Catholic Educational Association. This meeting stands in continuity with the proceedings of that committee.

After Kinshasha, the International Federation met in Salamanca, where a nucleus of theology chairmen from our various universities, together with others, decided to initiate some collaborative research among Catholic universities on subjects of interest to the kingdom. That initiative was followed up at our meeting last summer in Delhi, after an organizational gathering at the Catholic University in Washington under the leadership of President Walton. Out of all of that comes this meeting, where we are prepared to begin on a specific subject—well chosen, I think—to see what we might do to collaborate in our common concern for the kingdom of God on earth.

The service of Catholic institutions to the kingdom must be said to lie in their formal task of educating. This institution, for one, has 55,000 alumni, and I am sure that many of them are working day and night for the kingdom in many parts of the world. I see it all the time as I travel about, and I hear testimony of it from people who live and work with them. You could multiply that many thousands of times from the other institutions represented in this room. I believe that we are turning out people who are increasingly more competent and who are imbued with a sense of passion for the ills of our times, especially for those people who are left out or relegated to the fringes of society—the poor and the black and the Indian and the Chicano and, at times, the women among us. The people of the third and fourth worlds are also consciously in our concern, and I think that concern is felt more and more among those whom we educate. Finally, I think people tend to leave a Catholic institution with some sense of value that I would call a commitment to do something about creating a new world.

If I could step down a grade in higher education, we have found from a recent survey made here in conjunction with Rosemount College that a large number of the students we are receiving these days have had no parochial school education and consequently, very little religion. They hear a little bit about religion in their family, no doubt, but many do not have any Confraternity of Christian Doctrine exposure, and of course they hear nothing about religion in their public elementary and secondary schools. These young people come to us as what I would call theological illiterates. They simply don't know the common words like "gospel" or "epistle"; "incarnation," and "salvation," "redemption," and "the kingdom" are words that mean nothing to them. It is a sad situation, but I suppose one that might be expected in a highly secularized society. In the past we worried about indifference; today we worry about sheer ignorance of what I would call the religious reality. But we may assume that we can do something about that, and that all of us in Catholic higher education are doing something about it.

This meeting is more concerned with another aspect of the university or of the higher learning: research. Having vindicated our mission to our satisfaction and to the satisfaction (as far as I can understand) of Cardinal Garrone and all of those who are concerned about these matters in Rome, and certainly to the satisfaction of our own hierarchy, let us assume that we know what we are and what we are about. It is time, then, to see what we can do to be of service to the Church and the kingdom. Someone has said that the Catholic university is a place where the Church can do its thinking. It's a place where the Church can meet the secular world with all of its problems. It's a place where we can discuss many subjects which were only briefly touched upon in the Constitution on the Church in the Modern World. That document asked more questions than it gave answers, yet it remains our agenda for many years to come and could be a preparation for the next general council. Allow me to put down a few of these questions here, to prime the pump, as it were, about the kinds of concerns that should claim our attention in this meeting.

First, I believe that everything we do in an institution of Catholic higher learning should be carried out in an atmosphere of transcendence. We do admit that there is a God, and that he entered history through Christ becoming incarnate. We do agree that no matter what subjects we discuss, if they are of human value, they are also of divine value. By the very fact of becoming incarnate, Christ gave to all of humanity and everything human a tinge of divinity. Consequently, we do not want to discuss vexing human problems in the absence of faith and the faith commitment. Furthermore, in our institutions value is something one explicitly must talk about. Otherwise we fail our own tradition in its central conviction that we do whatever we do in the context of our faith and its most fundamental beliefs about man and God in this world.

There are so many other concerns that tumble one upon each other: problems of war and peace and nonviolence, as well as conscience in the face of violence. A whole spate of moral problems relate to marriage and family life, each of which looms larger today in the context of issues like population, abortion, cloning and the rest. Problems of value focus on the notion of justice: on the broadest scale, world justice which is seen in world hunger and world poverty and other deprivations of so many hundreds of millions of people who do not have the minimal physical conditions required even to begin to discuss human dignity. Questions of civil rights of all varieties in our own country and in many other countries of the world where they are cruelly denied today—even Catholic countries like Brazil and Chile. Questions of racial justice in our own country, justice tinged by color and often denied because of color. You know of all these problems. I find our students are increasingly concerned about all of them and do want to be involved in finding some kind of answers that we can live with as Christian humanists.

There is of course the large issue of ecumenism, ebbing and flowing in our times following the council; ebbing rather than flowing today, I think. There is the question of ecumenism among Christians with all of the attendant problems, liturgical and otherwise, that go with it. There are opportunities for ecumenism in the broader world society: a society that involves religions of the the book, like Islam and Judaism and ourselves; ecumenism with other great religions that involve hundreds of millions of people, like Buddhism, Hinduism, and the rest. There are enormous problems concerning human development in the world: development that is not looked upon as solely economic but broadly human, development that is social and cultural, religious and educational, yet economic as well, in the full span of justice.

There are problems in our own country with the notion of citizenship. What does it mean to be a good citizen in America today, especially in a bicentennial year? Do we revise history or do we try to get back to the original ideals and aspirations that gave us birth? Pat Moynihan recently remarked that patriotism is in tatters, that everything involving patriotism and the flag is either battered or banal or both. The basic legal question of church and state is a thorny one today: how much can the state impose upon the privacy of human beings and how much can it restrict the actions of people concerned about the kingdom and about conscience? These questions demand scrutiny by keen legal research, so they are very much the concern of the universities. A whole range of problems involve freedom and authority. A very wise Frenchman once said that liberty works if you live in a highly disciplined society. But freedom and authority too often work against each other: the individual versus the conventional conscience or the current authority. Questions of faith and reason remain a perennial one for Catholic universities, as do questions of faith and science.

Finally there are issues that affect us more closely as Christian human beings: prayer and the meaning of prayer, meditation and contemplation in modern life. Liturgy raises difficulties especially since we have set ourselves the task of evolving a liturgy that is to reflect the times in the images, words and aspirations of people who pray together with us in our day. Problems with apostolate, ministry and evangelization will be addressed at this meeting. I could keep extending this list, but this was intended to be no more than a *tour d'horizon*.

The last think I want to do is to simply read for you the prayer for today's liturgy which I think is appropriate for this meeting. I don't think there was any collusion between this prayer and this day and Father Burrell and Sister Franzita's planning, but it's a good prayer for this day and I conclude my remarks by simply reciting it:

Father in heaven, you revealed Christ as your Son by the voice that spoke over the waters of the Jordan. May all who share in the Sonship of Christ follow in his path of service to man and reflect the glory of his kingdom even to the ends of the earth for he is Lord, forever and ever.

Thank you very much for coming.

Evangelization in the American Context
Most Rev. Joseph L. Bernardin

I

There is a risk in speaking about the importance of a gathering like this at its outset—the risk of seeming to predict results which remain to be achieved. And yet we are all aware that this symposium symbolizes something of enormous potential for our Church and our society. Different people might express it in different ways. For myself, I think it reasonable to suppose that our coming-together here, along with other recent and continuing developments in the Church, signals a movement in the relationship between the Catholic scholarly community and the bishops and pastors in the Church: a movement from détente to entente. I believe we share the conviction that this movement is timely and welcome.

Specifically, this occasion, together with other parallel happenings, marks a movement beyond generalized affirmations of mutual respect and good will on the part of the representatives of the magisterium on the one hand and the academic community on the other; and a movement even beyond abstract formulations of the complementary roles and relationships of scholars and bishops. Neither of these things— affirmations of good will and attempts to define our relationship—has been put entirely behind us. It is important that they not be. But having affirmed our mutual respect in unmistakable terms, and having reflected at length in recent years upon our relationship, we are now able to come together to explore ways in which we can collaborate in confronting a major practical issue facing the Church in our nation: the challenge of evangelization in the American context.

It is entirely fitting that we should seek to concretize our relationship around this issue. As Pope Paul reminded all members of the Church in his Apostolic Exhortation on evangelization, proclaiming the Good News is not optional for any of us, not a task which the Church can take up or put aside at its discretion. "It is the duty incumbent on her by the command of the Lord Jesus, so that people can believe and be saved. This [gospel] message is indeed necessary. It is unique. It cannot be replaced. . . . It is a question of people's salvation" (*Evangelii Nuntiandi*, 5). Let us pray that our deliberations here may contribute to the Church's more perfect response to the mandate to evangelize.

As I have suggested, however, it would be premature to suppose that the working relationship of Catholic scholarship (of which I take Catholic higher education to be an essential institutional embodiment) and the magisterium has been definitively worked out. It would be unwise to postpone our efforts at concrete collaboration until it has been—for that might entail a very long postponement indeed. But it would also be unwise of us, in collaborating, to ignore the question of our mutual, complementary roles. Hence I wish this evening essentially to do two things: first, to sketch a few general notions which may prove helpful to our continuing efforts to define this critically important relationship; second, to propose a few topics for our agenda with respect to evangelization. There is a dynamic connection between the two which makes it logical and fruitful to proceed in this way.

II

It is a truism that the magisterium and the scholarly community have distinct but complementary roles. The question is not whether this is so, but what it means in practice. Much extremely useful thought has been given to this question in recent years, but I think it obvious that the question—at least in its practical aspects—is a long way from being answered conclusively. This should not cause us dismay or discouragement. The question is, after all, a perennial one. True, it has been raised in a sometimes acute form in recent years; even, at times, in the mode of contestation. Yet, to the extent that this has obliged us to recognize some longstanding but basically unacceptable ambiguities, the experience may ultimately prove to be beneficial.

For the sake of clarity, I should note that I understand the magisterium in the sense given the term by Vatican II. First, with respect to function: "The task of authentically interpreting the word of God, whether written or handed on, has been entrusted exclusively to the living teaching office of the Church, whose authority is exercised in the name of Jesus Christ'' (*Dei Verbum*, 10). Second, with respect to agents: "Bishops, teaching in communion with the Roman Pontiff, are to be respected by all as witnesses to divine and Catholic truth. In matters of faith and morals, the bishops speak in the name of Christ and the faithful are to accept their teaching and adhere to it with a religious assent of soul. This religious submission of will and of mind must be shown in a special way to the authentic teaching authority of the Roman Pontiff, even when he is not speaking ex cathedra. That is, it must be shown in such a way that his supreme magisterium is acknowledged with reverence, the judgments made by him are sincerely adhered to, according to his manifest mind and will'' (*Lumen Gentium*, 25). While working out the practical implications of these principles can be a complex matter, it is essential that we take such principles as fundamental.

I do not suggest that every ambiguity concerning the relationship between the magisterium and scholarship—any more than every ambiguity in any other area of life— can be totally resolved. But that is no reason to tolerate more ambiguity than is necessary or healthy. One source of confusion in the relationship between scholarship and the magisterium has been an occasional failure, on both sides, to distinguish clearly the kinds of issues or questions to which both are called to address themselves in different ways. At least three occur to me: those which are primarily doctrinal; those which are primarily pastoral (or practical); and those one might call "mixed" questions, in which both doctrinal and pastoral elements are strongly present. Of course virtually any doctrinal question has pastoral implications—and vice versa. But the doctrinal element does predominate in some issues, the pastoral in others. And the stronger the pastoral element, the more leeway there is at times for responsible discussion and debate with respect to alternatives, or adaptations to specific concrete situations.

Similarly, it seems to me important to distinguish different kinds of answers which can be given to questions in the life of the Church. Without proposing to develop an exhaustive taxonomy, I believe that here, too, it is possible to identify at least three general categories: first, hypotheses; second, what one might call provisional answers—which yet may be part of the authentic teaching of the Church; third, final or definitive answers. No doubt others can introduce other shadings and nuances into the discussion.

Such remarks may seem rather meaninglessly abstract, but I am moving toward a practical point. It is this. We needlessly confuse our discussions of the relationship between the magisterium and scholarship

by failing at times to clarify properly the kinds of questions we are dealing with and the kinds of answers we are giving. It is true, of course, that, considering the limitations of human intelligence, a certain amount of such confusion is unavoidable. Still, none of us should be overly tolerant of confusion which exceeds what is necessary.

On the side of the magisterium, it seems to me that a source of confusion is, perhaps, the tendency at times to equate hypotheses and provisional answers with final answers. The root cause of the problem, I believe, is the human tendency to absolutize valid but essentially contingent responses to historically and culturally conditioned circumstances. To put it more simply, the life of the Church is an exceedingly rich mixture of the changeless, the changeable, and the changing. It is not always easy for bishops, or anyone else, to tell them apart. The discussions at Vatican II are proof of this. Yet it is vitally important that we continually make the effort to do so: not only so that we will be able to assert with greater clarity and conviction the permanence of what is changeless in the teaching and practice of the Church, but so that we will also at least be open to weighing the merits of proposals for change in what is basically changeable (although of course not necessarily *to be* changed simply because, in theory at least, *could be* changed).

On the part of the Catholic scholarly community, it seems to me that perhaps a source of confusion is the tendency to disregard or depreciate the value and necessity of provisional answers rendered in and for the Church by the magisterium, especially when those answers are presented as part of the Church's authentic (though not solemnly defined) teaching. It is entirely possible that this tendency, or something like it, may be built into the basic thrust of the scholarly enterprise itself. The dialectic of scholarship tends to see every provisional response to a question as only a stage on the way toward a final resolution of the question—a stage, moreover, to be gotten beyond as rapidly as possible. In theory, this is a reasonable mode of intellectual procedure (although not one to be adopted and pursued altogether without qualification); in practice, however, when applied too simplistically to the ongoing life of an institution or a community such as the Church, it can exacerbate tensions and lead to highly questionable conclusions in the area of pastoral—that is to say, practical—policy.

Thus, I submit that it would be a serious practical (if not also theoretical) mistake for scholars to suppose, or act as if they supposed, that whatever has not been formally "defined" in and for the Church is therefore subject to change and quite probably ripe to be changed. On the contrary, to return to my earlier terminology, even the so-called provisional answers of the magisterium should be approached with profound respect: not the respect accorded museum pieces, but the respect we assign to living elements in a living community. This, I believe, is essentially what the Second Vatican Council was saying when it declared that "bishops, teaching in communion with the Roman Pontiff, are to be respected by all as witnesses to divine and Catholic truth. In matters of faith and morals, the bishops speak in the name of Christ and the faithful are to accept their teaching and adhere to it with a religious assent of soul" (*Lumen Gentium*, 25). To say this is not, certainly, to preclude the role of scholarship in probing and weighing the authentic but provisional answers of those who speak for the magisterium and proposing other answers—and even other questions. It is simply to suggest, in a very general way, an appropriate attitude for scholarship in going about this work, especially when the particular answer or teaching at issue has held the field for a very long time.

III

As we continue our efforts to define more clearly the relationship of the Catholic scholarly community and the magisterium, it is also essential to keep before us a reasonably clear and unambiguous notion of complementarity, particularly complementarity in the work of arriving at magisterial teaching. No good purpose will be served, least of all the well-being of the Church as a whole, either by the kind of imperialism which would attempt to co-opt scholarship as a mere instrumentality of the magisterium, or the kind of secessionism which would assert an absolute divorce between the two and an absolute freedom from accountability on scholarship's part either to the magisterium or to the Church as a whole. Fortunately, we can take guidance in this area from the substantial amount of healthy collaboration which has already occurred and is occurring now between scholars and bishops. But the question remains an enormously complex one, and it is far easier in the abstract to say what should not be done than what should. Yet at least we may avoid certain more obvious mistakes by keeping such negative principles in mind. And we will also profit by bearing in mind that the word of God has been given to the whole Church, and both the representatives of the magisterium and scholars have a role to play in seeking to discern and express what has thus been communicated to the Church.

Some conclusions follow. One is that those most responsible for the magisterial function truly respect Catholic scholarship when it is functioning according to the norms of true scholarship. Among other things, scholarship has its own kinds of hypotheses and provisional answers; and, when these are recognized and treated on all sides for what they are, they should not only be tolerated but encouraged by representatives of the magisterium. Some will object that in this way errors will occur and the faithful will be scandalized; but errors will occur in any case, and, as far as scandal is concerned, it seems to me that no more harm (and quite probably less) will result from the mistaken hypotheses of scholars—provided they are presented as hypotheses—than from the stultification of scholarship.

At the same time, as a practical matter, it would be well if scholars, engaging in the legitimate work of formulating hypotheses with respect to issues in the life of the Church, paid more attention to the immediate practical consequences which such activity can have. Scholarship requires the free speculative exchange of ideas if it is to flourish. But, particularly in an age of rapid mass communications reaching persons who are often theologically unsophisticated, it seems to me that a sense of responsibility for the welfare of all the members of the Church makes doubly important the cultivation of such virtues as prudence, modesty, and a realistic sense of one's own limitations. We cannot allow the fear of giving scandal to paralyze us, but neither can we ignore the reality of scandal or fail to take reasonable precautions against allowing untested hypotheses to become normative for belief and action. If we are honest, we must admit that there have been times in the recent past when theological speculation has been immediately translated into pastoral practice. This has been a concern of the bishops, but it must also be a concern of the scholars.

There is a further obligation incumbent upon the scholarly community. It is to recognize that the magisterium is not simply an administrative convenience—much less an obstacle—in the Church, but is in fact a vital ministry of service within the Catholic community, intended for it by the will of its Founder. I do not mean in saying this to divinize the magisterium in its human, institutional embodiments. But I do contend, first, that even the human and institutional embodiments of the magisterium are not without their intrinsic importance, and, beyond that, that the magisterial function is not an historical accident but is, on the contrary, of the essence of the Christian Church.

Following upon this is another point which deserves comment in such a discussion as this. We have begun lately to hear talk of "multiple" magisteria in the Church. I confess, however, that I find the term ambiguous and even incorrect. Granted, we all have more to learn about the ways in which others besides the Pope and bishops contribute to the magisterial function in the Church; specifically, in the context of this symposium, I wish to affirm my conviction that we need to examine with the utmost seriousness the question of how theology and theologians fit in. But none of this, it seems to me, points at all to the conclusion that there are "multiple" magisteria. To suggest otherwise goes contrary to our understanding of the Church's teaching role and causes avoidable and potentially dangerous confusion. Furthermore, in the practical order, such a notion obscures and undermines valid complementarity—between the respective roles of the magisterium and the scholarly community—and at its worst could actually lead to painful and broadly destructive competition at the expense of the entire Church. I hasten to add that I do not believe anyone seriously desires this; I wish merely to make the cautionary observation that we should not allow ourselves to be seduced by defective verbal formulas into a competition which no one desires and from which no one will benefit.

IV

I wish now to turn to the question of topics for our agenda for evangelization in the American context. It is not difficult, to say the least, to find areas which invite reflection and action. This is so both because of the comprehensiveness of the Church's evangelizing mission and because of the many, urgent spiritual needs of contemporary society. With respect to the former, one need only recall Pope Paul's comment that if one had to express the purpose of evangelization in a single sentence, "the best way of stating it would be to say that the Church evangelizes when she seeks to convert, solely through the divine power of the Message she proclaims, both the personal and collective consciences of people, the activities in which they engage, and the lives and concrete milieux which are theirs" (*Evangelii Nuntiandi*, 18). This implies a program which challenges the very best of which we are capable.

I do not imagine that the two matters to which I wish to call your attention by any means exhaust the catalogue of the appropriate and necessary. It is simply that both seem to me exceptionally relevant to the present needs of the Church and society, and both have a strong bearing upon the task of evangelization in our nation at this moment. The first is the renewal of Christian ethics; the second is the development of a "foundational" theology or what some have called a "new apologetics." The contributions of the Catholic scholarly community are absolutely essential to both enterprises.

I addressed myself to the renewal of Christian ethics a year ago in a paper which some of you may have read. Nothing which has happened since then suggests any diminishing in the ethical crisis of American society. I shall not repeat the litany of disturbing disclosures and unresolved controversies over public and private morality which challenge us as a people. The evidence is overwhelming that ours is, morally speaking, a profoundly confused and deeply troubled society. Thus one must place the evangelization of the American value system high on the list of priorities for the Church as it reflects upon its responsibilities with respect to evengalization today.

Yet it is clear that the Church itself experiences confusion in this area. The inadequacy of both the "old" and the "new" moralities is widely recognized; but there is no consensus with regard either to ethical theory or the application of ethical norms to many specific cases. As I remarked a year ago: "Our need . . . is for a new 'new' morality which combines the best of the 'old' approach—its recognition of moral absolutes, its insistence on the need for moral norms, its delineation of definite content for charity—with the best of the 'new' approach—its insistence on the importance of the person, the context of action, and the primacy of charity in Christian moral living" ("What Can the Church Expect from Catholic Universities?" January 17, 1975). I am aware of and grateful for the serious rethinking of ethics now being pursued by many Catholic and Christian scholars. I strongly urge that these efforts be continued, while at the same time we seek earnestly for ways of relating these efforts more directly and collaboratively to the Church's magisterium, so as to make them more pertinent to the mission of evangelization.

Let me quote myself once more on this topic:

> . . . It is clear that the new "new morality" which I am urging cannot be derived from the "old" and "new" approaches simply by creating a patchwork or pastiche of ethical theories. The need rather is for a rigorous rethinking of moral theory and the development of an integral Christian ethic which, while incorporating the best of the "old" and the "new," is also something greater than the mere sum of its parts. Here, too, the contributions of Catholic higher

21

education and Catholic scholarship are indispensable. ("What Can the Church Expect from Catholic Universities?")

The second matter which I propose for our joint agenda is the development of a "new apologetics" or "foundational theology." It is a matter of growing urgency that we identify clearly and cogently the reasons for belief, without of course equating these with faith itself.

One of the most common mistakes people make about faith today is that it is simply something to be experienced, perhaps in a quasi-mystical manner, independently of a content of belief to be known and accepted by the intellect. This has many bad results. For one thing, it causes many intelligent but not especially "religious" people to look down on religion and not to take it seriously. This has been a serious problem in Western society for the past several centuries, and it continues to be a problem today. For another thing, it has the effect of cutting off many people from an authentic and important part of their intellectual and cultural heritage. Religious illiteracy is as real a problem in our country today as the illiteracy of reading and writing and spelling. And it is a pernicious thing because, naturally enough, people are not aware of what they do *not* know about religion. To the extent that this kind of illiteracy robs cultural life and public discourse of an important intellectual dimension, it makes living a bit more drab and, possibly, a bit more dangerous than it need be.

Nor should we deceive ourselves by supposing that this is not a problem for Catholics. It is difficult to disagree with Father Carl Peter's observation, in an address more than a year ago to the bishops, that "Catholics in increasing numbers (are) wondering *what* to believe and more yet why"; and that, as a result, "it is no easy thing to attain or to maintain the conviction that is required for anything like permanent commitment." Thus one must also accept the validity of his appeal for the development of a foundational theology, or "new apologetics," adequate to the needs of our times and our people:

We mightily need a solid effort to articulate the reasons for believing as a Christian today. Apologetics was too often polemical and offensive in the past. Today we require something notably different. [Parenthetically, it also seems appropriate that we follow up on his suggestion that this issue be placed on the agenda of Christian ecumenism.] But we do need an effort to make an honest case for believing and for faith—this from educated men and women, lay and cleric, who are committed both to their Christian faith and to the unbending demands of critical intelligence. . . . Christian faith needs a systematic effort made to state not only what the basic teachings are but what they have to commend them as true and as beneficial to believer and non-believer alike (Rev. Carl Peter, "Renewal of Faith and Beliefs," November 17, 1975).

V

In concluding these remarks, I wish very briefly to reflect upon the broad social and cultural context within which the Church must carry on the work of evangelization today. Here, too, I find valuable a comment by Father Peter: "Beliefs are expressed in symbols, language, and concepts profoundly influenced by culture. When the convictions regarding the criteria of truth and value that are central to a culture are called into question, then attention should be given to beliefs. Otherwise they may be rejected along with the culture in terms of which they were formed and articulated" (*Ibid.*)

Not just our nation but our world is today experiencing a profound crisis of culture. This has been analyzed in various ways, and among the analyses which deserve our attention is that of Christopher Dawson. Dawson wrote often of the secularization of Western society, the divorce between religion and culture, as an underlying cause of contemporary problems. But it is important to recall that he did not consider secularization an essentially contemporary phenomenon. Rather, he traced its occurrence back at least two centuries, and argued that something quite different from—although not unrelated to—secularization was occurring now: the collapse of the secularized substitute for Christianity which had become dominant in Western culture even before the French Revolution. As he put it:

> For a generation—during the last third of the 18th century—the Religion of Nature became a real religion and no mere ideological fantasy, a faith in which men believed with their whole souls and for which they were prepared to die. In spite of the vagueness of its beliefs—its faith in progress, its hope in the coming of an age of social perfec-

tion and universal happiness, its optimistic faith in a providential order of nature, its belief in Democracy and the doctrine of political freedom, social equality and spiritual fraternity—it would be a mistake to underestimate its religious character, since it continued to be the dominant creed for a great part of Western civilization down to the beginning of the 20th century. Indeed the present spiritual crisis of our culture is due not so much to the loss of the traditional faith in Christianity, which had already occurred by the time of the French Revolution, as to the collapse of this new religion which has occurred in the present century, especially after two world wars (*The Dividing of Christendom*, New York, 1965, p. 268).

Relating this to Father Peter's comment, it may not be too wide of the mark to say that for the past two centuries Christianity has been a tolerated, if not precisely welcomed, part of the cultural apparatus of secularized, humanistic Western society. Now that culture appears to be in confusion and disarray. With respect to the Church and its mission of evangelization, this presents both a danger and an opportunity: a danger if, by inaction or ineptness, we allow the fate of Christianity to be determined (humanly and relatively speaking) by the fate of a particular culture; an opportunity if we are able to demonstrate the total relevance of the gospel message, not only to a particular human culture, but more importantly to human life in every culture and every age.

This will make enormous demands on us, demands which we must meet together, lest we fail to meet them at all. Our reasons for doing so are many; but it is well that we reflect upon the words of Pope Paul:

Men can gain salvation also in other ways, by God's mercy, even though we do not preach the Gospel to them; but as for us, can we gain salvation if through negligence or fear or shame—what Saint Paul called ''blushing for the gospel''—or as a result of false ideas we fail to preach it? For that would be to betray the call of God, who wishes the seed to bear fruit through the voice of the ministers of the Gospel (*Evangelii Nuntiandi*, 80).

II. GENERAL SESSIONS
January 12

The Pastoral Issues:
The Point of View of the Church
Most Rev. Bernard F. Law

The opening prayer for the Epiphany frames my thought and hope for our coming together:

> Father of light, unchanging God,
> today you reveal to men of faith
> the resplendent fact of the Word made flesh.
> Your light is strong,
> your love is near;
> draw us beyond the limits which this world imposes,
> to the life where your Spirit makes all life complete.
> We ask this through Christ our Lord.

These remarks will be based on my pastoral experience, brief as it is. This will of necessity be a very personal statement. It is offered to you in the hope that it might help us to come more quickly to fruitful discussion—as a point of departure, of convergence, or of divergence. I wish that these remarks carried the weight of scholarship. Its absence points to a way in which Catholic universities and colleges might assist the mission of the Church in smaller dioceses. Would it be possible to develop the ministry of a scholar, a theologian, a research assistant in residence to assist bishops and their staffs in dioceses without institutions of higher learning? Before leaving this point, let me indicate my willingness to pursue this possibility with any interested university or college president!

Our Holy Father has given us, in his recent Exhortation on Evangelization in the Modern World, a graced document eloquently and movingly illuminating the theme of this symposium. He writes:

> ... The Good News of the Kingdom which is coming and which has begun is meant for all people of all times. Those who have received the Good News and who have been gathered by it into the community of salvation can and must communicate and spread it. The Church knows this. She has a vivid awareness of the fact that the Savior's words, ''I must proclaim the Good News of the kingdom of God,'' apply in all truth to herself. .... It is a task and mission which the vast and profound changes of present-day society make all the more urgent. Evangelizing is in fact the grace and vocation proper to the Church, her deepest identity. She exists in order to evangelize ... (*Evangelii Nuntiandi*, 13, 14).

In isolating the key pastoral issues for the Church today, the general rubric I will use is evangelization. The richness of the theme is borne witness to by the 1974 Synod of Bishops. Drawing as he does upon the insights of that Synod, the Holy Father writes in his Exhortation:

> Evangelization, as we have said, is a complex process made up of varied elements: the renewal of humanity, witness, explicit proclamation, inner adherence, entry into the community, acceptance of signs, apostolic initiative. These elements may appear to be contradictory, indeed mutually exclusive. In fact they are complementary and mutually enriching. Each one must always be seen in relationship with the others. The value of the last Synod was to have constantly invited us to relate these elements rather than to place them in opposition one to the other, in order to reach a full understanding of the Church's evangelizing activity (*Evangelii Nuntiandi*, 24).

We need, as a Church, to reflect together more deeply on the implications of our mission to evangelize—on the full scope of the mandate which is ours to go out to the whole world and make disciples of all nations. The narrow vision must be avoided. Our prayer is that the

Father of light would draw us beyond the limits which the world imposes.

Ours is, and is called to be, a Church catholic—a Church universal. The temptation is upon us constantly to restrict our world to manageable units, to logically coherent systems. Our birthright as a people, however, is rooted in the limitless mystery of God's love revealed in Jesus Christ. Whatever it is that we may be able to say about God, there is infinitely more drawing us beyond our thought to communion with him.

The Holy Father, reflecting on our moment in history, writes: "We live in the Church at a privileged moment of the Spirit" (*Evangelii Nuntiandi*, 75). These words are not simply a rhetorical bridge to link two thoughts, but rather a faith-filled observation about our day. And what is the work of the Spirit if not to bestow and evoke within us that freedom and confidence which allows us to cry out Abba, Father?

The coming of the Spirit upon the Church at Pentecost transformed the reticent and fearful hearts of the disciples through the power of Christ's cross and resurrection. The world, waiting to be renewed, re-created, to have the gospel preached to it, was the same before the Pentecostal experience as it was after; the need for God's healing word was equally present. The impulse to evangelize did not come from without in terms of those in need; it came from within in terms of the power of God at work in the Church through the Spirit.

That same power is at work in us. Paul, in his letter to the Ephesians, writes to us as well when he says:

To the saints who are also faithful in Christ Jesus:
Grace to you and peace from God our Father and the
    Lord Jesus Christ.
Blessed be the God and Father of our Lord Jesus Christ,
who has blessed us in Christ with every spiritual
    blessing. . . .
He destined us in love to be his sons through Jesus Christ,
according to the purpose of his will, to the praise of
his glorious grace which he freely bestowed on us
    in the beloved.
He has made known to us in all wisdom and insight the
mystery of his will, according to the purpose which he
set forth in Christ as a plan for the fullness of time,
to unite all things in him, things in heaven and things
on earth (Ephesians 1 and 2).

Here, surely, meditating with Paul on the mystery of his will, we are drawn beyond the limits which this world imposes.

In his Exhortation the Holy Father says: "The Church remains in the world when the Lord of glory returns to the Father. She remains as a sign—simultaneously obscure and luminous—of a new presence of Jesus, of his departure and of his permanent presence. She prolongs and continues him. And it is above all his mission and his condition of being an evangelizer that she is called upon to continue" (*Evangelii Nuntiandi*, 15).

We have a great need in the Church at all levels to reflect prayerfully and together upon the radical dimension of our common mission which is to evangelize the world. To get at this mission in a pastoral way, the words of the Holy Father provide a key when he says: "The Church is an evangelizer, but she begins by being evangelized herself. She is

> the community of believers,
> the community of hope lived and communicated,
> the community of brotherly love;
> and she needs to listen unceasingly to
>   what she must believe,
> to her reasons for hoping,
> to the new commandment of love.

"She is the People of God immersed in the world, and often tempted by idols, and she always needs to hear the proclamation of the 'mighty works of God' which converted her to the Lord; she always needs to be called together afresh by him and reunited" (*Evangelii Nuntiandi*, 15).

To be sure, we are never beyond the need of renewal this side of the eschaton, just as we will never have passed beyond our need to be evangelized as Church. It would be evasive of the demands of mission if we were to defer outreach on the basis of our internal shortcomings. With this understanding, my focus will be, as it has been, on our need to be evangelized as a condition for a more effective witness in the world.

"The Church is the community of believers." To affirm and to realize this note of the Church is a major pastoral concern today. The Church is the community of *believers*. "You are no longer strangers and sojourners, but you are fellow citizens with the saints and members of the household of God, built upon the foundation of the apostles and prophets, Christ Jesus himself being the cornerstone, in whom the whole structure is joined together and grows into a holy temple in the

Lord; in whom you also are built into it for a dwelling place of God in the Spirit'' (Ephesians 2:2–22).

Jesus' witness to himself as the Way, the Truth, and the Life, must resonate not only in our personal lives but in our life together as Church. The climate of unbelief, of suspended belief, of practical atheism, of the drama of atheistic humanism (cf. Henri de Lubac, *Le drame de l'humanisme athée,* ed. Spes, Paris, 1945—cited in *Evangelii Nuntiandi,* 55), the privileged position of secularism as almost the established religion of our land, the restrictive forces of the consumer society, the pursuit of the pleasure principle, the drive for power and domination, the pervasive presence of discrimination all bind the human spirit and make faith difficult.

Yet, the Father of light, the unchanging God, has revealed to us the resplendent fact of the Word made flesh. The Word is light from light. The condition for our bearing witness to the light is that we first be illumined by the strength of that light. Before we can magnify his presence in power and love to the world we must have a singular, concentrated focus on that primordial resplendent fact of faith that the Word was made flesh and dwelt among us.

I find the observations of Cardinal Suenens to the point when he says:

> We have been occupied with revising the structures of the Church at many levels. This was necessary, and the enterprise is far from completion. However, today the very foundations of the faith are questioned. And yet the Church has meaning only in Christ. And Christ has meaning only if he is the Son of God. And God has meaning only if he is the living and personal God. But, alas, all this has become problematic. . . .
>
> Many must be helped to exchange a sociological Christianity for a full and active life of faith. Christianity which we have inherited, which has its foundation mainly in the family and education, must mature into a Christianity of choice, based on a personal decision and embraced with full consciousness. . . .
>
> This is at the heart of our pastoral problems: the glaring contrast between the nominal and the authentic Christian'' (Leon Joseph Suenens, *A New Pentecost,* pp. 123, 124).

How do we become more clearly, more consciously a community of believers? How do we discern and maintain the delicate balance between the image of this faith community as a leaven in society and the call to this community of faith to be prophet, to be a voice crying in the wilderness? What does it mean for us today to be in the world but not of it? To be a community of believers is to imply a canon of judgment, is to imply a concept of right and wrong, is to resist absorption. The ultimate norm is, for the believer, Jesus Christ.

Our identity as a community, as well as our identity as individuals, is rooted in Jesus Christ. However supportive may have been the family, the school, the neighborhood for the Church, and we do well to do all that is possible to evangelize these as well as all of society, this word of Jesus is a sobering corrective against misplaced emphases or loyalties:

> I have come to set a man against his father, and a daughter against her mother, and a daughter-in-law against her mother-in-law, and man's foes will be those of his own household. He who loves father or mother more than me is not worthy of me; and he who loves son or daughter more than me is not worthy of me; and he who does not take up his cross and follow me is not worthy of me. He who finds his life will lose it, and he who loses his life for my sake will find it (Matthew 10:35–38).

We are called to be a *community* of believers. There is a holy interdependence characterizing our lives together as a community of faith. We are graced with an interdependence which transcends the suspicion, hostility, fear, and drive to domination which the world sets as limiting boundaries to human relationships. We *are* one in faith. What we *shall* be has not yet been revealed. The mystery of our life as community, signed and strengthened preeminently in Eucharist, is all too often obscured from our consciousness.

How can we be more consciously a community of believers? Enriched as we are by a renewed appreciation of the diversity which our unity can sustain, we can also too easily make idols of a legitimate point of view, a legitimate theological emphasis, a legitimate pastoral approach. However valid the idea may be in itself, it takes on a demonic force when it becomes the matrix for division within the Church. A community which finds and expresses its unity in Eucharist cannot, with integrity to itself, become a collectivity of hostile and mutually suspicious factions. This sometimes happens, and whenever it does, there we see clearly the Church's need to be evangelized.

Obviously I am not implying that *what* we believe is unimportant—

for our identity as a community is established in a common belief in Jesus Christ. What I am saying is that our one affirmation of faith should free us from the limits set by the world for human relationships, enabling us to live community in mutual trust, respect, love.

Our coming together here affirms our desire to do just that. To be sure, the responsibilities of the college and university president and that of bishop vary. The academic community is by nature a restricted community. Most members of that community are transitional. The service to truth in the academic community is often at the horizon of our theological understanding. The pastoral care of the bishop embraces the whole Church throughout the lives of each member and, while fostering theological development, is charged with handing on the faith of our fathers unimpaired. That there have been moments of negative conflict between segments of the Catholic academic community and some bishops is obvious to all of us. That there should be such conflict I refuse to accept as axiomatic. This is not to say that a certain constructive tension will not be part of our shared life. It remains constructive, however, only as long as its resolution is found in expression and experience of our community as believers—preeminently in Eucharist.

The Catholic academic community remains Catholic, or so it must to maintain its integrity. It must both remain and become Catholic. I hope and pray that this symposium will contribute to the desire of many in the Church for a clearer unity of vision shared by bishops and the Catholic academic community.

If I have spoken of community as lived by bishops and Catholic academic institutions, it is not to say there are not problems in this area elsewhere in the Church. For better or for worse, the parish is the place where most Catholics encounter the community of believers. At the November 1975 meeting of the National Conference of Catholic Bishops, Bishop Albert H. Ottenweiler expressed the conviction of many when he asked for study of alternate "models" of the parish in order to achieve more community in parish life. The growing interest in subcommunities, the flourishing of such groups as Cursillo, prayer groups, and Marriage Encounter speak to us, it seems to me, of a growing need in the Church for more opportunities for more Catholics to experience Church as a *community* of believers. Catholic academic communities, no less than other subcommunities in the Church, should become more fully communities of believers. Here is the model freeing Catholic educational institutions from the limits which the world imposes.

Our Holy Father reminds the Church in his Exhortation:

> "The Lord's spiritual testament tells us that unity among his
> followers is not only the proof that we are his, but also the
> proof that he is sent by the Father. It is the test of the
> credibility of Christians and of Christ himself. As
> evangelizers, we must offer Christ's faithful not the image
> of people divided and separated by unedifying quarrels, but
> the image of people who are mature in faith and capable of
> finding a meeting-point beyond the real tensions, thanks to a
> shared, sincere and disinterested search for truth. Yes, the
> destiny of evangelization is certainly bound up with the
> witness of unity given by the Church. This is a source of
> responsibility and also of comfort" (*Evangelii Nuntiandi*,
> 77).

The Church is called to be a community of hope lived and communicated. We give thanks to God for the hopeful vision of Pope John XXIII
when he said in his opening speech to the Second Vatican Council,
"We feel we must disagree with those prophets of gloom, who are
always forecasting disaster, as though the end of the world were at
hand." Whether ours are the worst of days or the best of days I have
neither the ability nor the inclination to determine. In the final analysis,
such speculation is beside the point, because the motive for our hope
does not spring from the age in which we live—it is rooted in Calvary's
Hill and springs from the death and resurrection of Jesus Christ. The
Church affirms, in the face of each night, this hope-filled word:

> In the tender compassion of our God
> the dawn from on high shall break upon us,
> to shine on those who dwell in darkness
>   and in the shadow of death,
> and to guide our feet into the way of peace.
>   (Luke 1:78, 79)

That we face in our nation, not to say throughout the world, great
obstacles to the Church's mission goes without saying.

Our hope, however, is in the resplendent fact of the Word made flesh,
in the brightness of his light, in the nearness of his love.

We are called to communicate that hope in our life of communion with him in the Spirit and through him with one another. To be able to illumine the darkness of death, of despair, of loneliness with the dawn of a new day, of the eternal day—is to live in hope. To be signs of hope, to be a constellation of stars illuminating his presence in our midst is to be a community of hope lived and communicated.

And finally, the Church is called to be a community of brotherly love. The greatest of these is love. ''I give you a new commandment: Love one another. Such as my love has been for you, so must your love be for each other. This is how all will know you for my disciples: your love for one another'' (John 13:34–35).

The bishops of the United States, in their collective pastoral, *To Teach as Jesus Did,* reflect on this passage and its meaning for us as community:

> As God's plan unfolds in the life of an individual Christian, he grows in awareness that, as a child of God, he does not live in isolation from others. From the moment of Baptism he becomes a member of a new and larger family, the Christian community. Reborn in Baptism, he is joined to others in common faith, hope and love. This community is based not on force or accident of geographic location or even on deeper ties of ethnic origin, but on the life of the Spirit which unites its members in a unique fellowship so intimate that Paul likens it to a body of which each individual is a part and Jesus himself is the Head. In this community one person's problem is everyone's problem and one person's victory is everyone's victory. Never before or never since the coming of Jesus Christ has anyone proposed such a community (*To Teach as Jesus Did*, 22).

To sing the praises of this reality is one thing; to incarnate it is something else again. Yet that is what we must do. How can we, as Church, be more responsive to the needs of one another within the community? How can we broaden our vision, transcend the limits set by the world, and live a life of loving service for others? What are the implications of love in the face of world hunger, the consumer society, the drive for power and domination in individuals, in nations, and in groups of nations, nuclear armaments, personal and political exploitation? How do we express our love in service through the varied structures of the Church as well as in our personal lives?

To be Church is to have the compassion and gentle sensitivity of Jesus for the multitude. To live the mystery of Church is to be Sacrament of Christ's presence, to be Communion, to be Herald, to be Servant, and to be all this in and through the structures of institution. The critical pastoral issues, as I see them, revolve around the nature of the Church to be Community of believers, of hope, and of love, and the Church's mission to evangelize and her call to be evangelized. It is within this framework that I would situate more specific pastoral issues.

Christian Scholars and the Work of the Church

John T. Noonan, Jr.

We meet this afternoon to consider concrete ways in which Catholics who are scholars can contribute to the mission of the Church. That mission, as we are reminded by *Gaudium et spes*, includes both internal development and service to human beings outside the Christian community,[1] so that Catholic scholars contribute to it either when they increase the Church's self-awareness of identity, purposes, and potentialities, or when they enlarge the general human understanding of the human person's identity, purposes, and potentialities. We are meeting at a time when the International Federation of Catholic Universities has laid down a broad agenda for interdisciplinary research by Catholic scholars; when the senior staff of the National Catholic Conference of Catholic Bishops has specified, in an American context, the areas where research is needed; and when the President and the General Secretary of the episcopal body have issued an invitation to scholars to collaborate in the work of the Church.[2]

Why has there been this recent interest and these recent invitations? In part, because the Church is emerging from the Tridentine fortress, and to reach men and women in the larger world the Church's old methods are ineffective; in part, because in the wake of Vatican II, the old ways of doing ecclesiology and moral theology have become inadequate. Before 1965 the specific areas in which research has now been called for—the ministries, sacraments and structure of the Church; Christian life and the family; the Church in the contemporary world—these areas would have been considered the province of the ecclesiologist, the dogmatic theologian, and the moralist. But it is evi-

---

[1]Second Vatican Council, *Constitutio pastoralis de ecclesia in mundo huius temporis*, Prooemium.

[2]Inter-University Committee on Research and Policy Studies, *Newsletter*, vol. 1., December 5, 1975.

dent that these specialists do not possess the techniques or the wisdom to deal with the problems of these areas today. In the past the bishops as a body have turned to the theologians of the Catholic University of America, while individual bishops looked to the theologians at their seminaries or at the theologates of the religious orders. Today the bishops have expanded their consultors to include the Catholic scholars of the country.

I propose this afternoon to do four things: First, to review and set aside a variety of ways in which the tasks before us might be accomplished. Second, to put before you what seem to me the best existing examples of research aiding the mission of the Church. Third, to say what academically may be expected of scholars engaged in such work and the moral risks of their enterprise. Fourth, to give one hypothetical example of scholarship from a Christian perspective reorienting a general discipline. I shall raise some questions as I go, and implicit in each example will be questions you may wish to answer otherwise.

The appeals of the Catholic universities and the American bishops call for a response. Shall that response involve all 240 Catholic colleges and 100 seminaries; should it depend only on the forty Catholic universities and dozen theologates; should it be borne in part by Catholic faculty at the secular institutions? With all of these Catholic scholars in existence, there has been an understandable desire to tap what is, as it were, already in place. Let me voice the counter opinion. As the survey research of Ladd and Lipset has demonstrated, "American academics constitute a teaching profession, not a scholarly one."[3] Only four percent of American faculty members identify themselves as having heavy research interests.[4] A number of these have interests in fields from particle physics to zoology, which are remote from the present areas of research important to the Church. A number of these have no interest in the Church. Those with relevant research interests with a commitment to the Church are a small fraction of the four percent substantially involved in research. The actual pool of available research scholars for our enterprise is small.

To rely for research on everyone and every institution engaged in the common work of Christian education is to indulge in makework. An enterprise of that kind requires coordinators and committees. No committee is stronger than its chairman, no consultation better than its

---

[3]"The 1975 Ladd-Lipset Survey of U.S. Faculty Members", *Chronicle of Higher Education*, vol. 11, p. 2, October 14, 1975.
[4]*Idem.*

coordinators. Weekend colloquia are no substitute for explorations in depth. Conferences, consultations, committees tincture the theological problem areas with academic coloring; they do not transform them.

It is always possible, no doubt, to hire bright people to spend their time thinking about your shortand intermediate-range problems. It may be possible to enlist some in the service of the Church as they are sometimes enlisted in the service of the Bureau of the Budget or the Solicitor General's office. It might be possible to organize a number of them into a kind of ecclesiastical Rand Corporation, bringing the most advanced techniques of maximization strategy to bear on the immediate concerns of the American Church. I do not mean to disparage the exploration of national strategies for the attainment of limited goals. Even the education of a few bishops-to-be at institutes of policy studies would be beneficial to the administration of the Church, as the Canon Law Society of America has already said. But Rand-type research by scholars on assignment involves a substantial mixture of scholarship with political judgment as to what the client wants and what the immediate situation permits. As to the great problem areas of the Church, her ministries, sacraments, structures, and functions in the modern world, and Christian life and the family, the research needed is fundamental and cannot be left to strategists.

Do we need, then, an Institute of Advanced Studies or a Center for Advanced Research in the Theological Sciences? Both models have their attractions. Adopting the model of the Institute, we would seek to bring together in a single place established scholars chosen from theology and the other apposite fields who would pursue their own research interests. Such an Institute would have the inestimable benefit of concentrating intellectual effort. I reject it as insufficiently focused and too open to the dangers of mandarinism on which I will enlarge. It would, moreover, be expensive: for twenty scholars an endowment of $25 million would be a minimum. (I speak in American, not European terms where money is concerned.) The alternative model, the Center, supposes a yearly rotation of selected fellows in theology and the related social sciences and humanities. It is far better than the weekend or four-day conference in permitting continued dialogue among colleagues from diverse specialities; well-executed, it is bound to aid in the crossing of disciplinary boundaries and the diffusion of leading concepts; it does not have the disadvantage of setting up a permanently picked and isolated elite. It can succeed with, say, twelve fellows a year, on an annual budget of at least $750,000 or an endowment of $15 million; a single scholar-administrator; and expert panels to choose each year's crop of fellows. But while I should expect such a form to be a remarkable addition to Catholic and ecumenical scholarship, it would not fulfill the function of sustained research in the great problem areas.

What is needed in response to the university presidents and the bishops is not an enterprise with democratic participation, bureaucratically coordinated. What is needed most is not an Institute beyond our present means nor a Center perfecting the interchange of ideas. Let us ask instead, what are the best existing models for the performance of serious scholarly work at costs which do not exceed available resources?

Do we have at hand any model where a traditional field of theological expertise has been enlarged to include the data and methodology of other specialities, where the field has been renewed and transformed so that in 1976 it bears little resemblance to what it was in 1900, where major scholarly work has opened ecumenical doors and enlarged the Church's own self-understanding? I believe we do. It is in scriptural studies, where archeological, linguistic, and historical data and methodologies have been successfully integrated with doctrinal analysis, where almost everything that was taken for granted in 1900 has been revised or abandoned, where the work of the scholars has reached out to the Protestants and led the Church to a new consciousness of the birth and early years of the Christian community.

These accomplishments were largely due to the pioneering work of a few men, preeminent among them Marie-Joseph Lagrange. There were those who thought the task of integrating contemporary scholarship and faith impossible. Some of these like Loisy despaired and defected. Others chose to remain in the Church and to attack the scholarship. The Pontifical Biblical Commission in its early years acted as a harsh monitor of orthodoxy. Despite disheartening defections and surveillance, Lagrange and his collaborators persevered. Their work took institutional shape in the École Biblique at Jerusalem. It found expression in 1892 in the *Revue Biblique* which was followed ten years later by the *Biblische Zeitschrift* and—it is painful to confess—over forty-seven years later by the *Catholic Biblical Quarterly*, the first specialized journal of scriptural studies edited by English-speaking Catholics. After a half century of effort, Lagrange's work received public papal acceptance in 1943 in the encyclical *Divino afflante spiritu*. Another twenty years later, the flowering of scriptural scholarship was evident at Vatican II and in the new relations with the Protestant Churches.

I do not find in this history any reason to suppose that the acceptance of scholarly work in the Church is automatic or easy. Nor do I believe that the integration of biblical scholarship with the life of the Church has been perfectly achieved. The necessary effort to maintain the integrity of their own discipline has sometimes led individual biblical scholars to disdain or at least disregard the larger Christian community in which alone the words of scripture live. We feel that lack of integration when a narrow literalism in translation ignores the place of scripture in the liturgy; or when a historical exegesis of a text on social conduct is made into a norm of Christian behavior, as though Christian experience had no part to play in the Church's understanding of a moral injunction. These imperfections arise from the difficulty of bringing a partial science into a whole of many sciences and a way of life.

What made the major positive achievement possible was three things: the utter dedication of a few; the creation of special institutes to provide centers for their work; and the diffusion of their ideas by books and learned journals. If you seek a model by which scholarship may serve the mission of the Church, Lagrange and the École Biblique furnish the finest example.

You may observe three features of this model. First, it suggests that basic research is done by highly motivated and gifted individuals with a few collaborators whose primary responsibility is not teaching; it is helped by some corporate form, not that of a university. Second, the theological faculties of the seminaries and universities were eventually won over to the new scholarship; they did not initiate it; they did provide an indispensable audience. Third, an official body outside the field was needed to legitimize the work in the Church as a whole; the Pontifical Biblical Commission ultimately performed this function.

Do we have a model of Catholic scholarship directed more to the service of man in general than to the internal consciousness of the Church, an example of research by Catholics which has transformed a field of knowledge so that man knows his potentialities more deeply and grasps his identity more fully? Biblical studies deal with the work of man but also in a special way with the work of God. Are there less sacred areas illuminated by the research of Catholics? The Middle Ages, of course, have often been seen as a Catholic era because of the social dominance of ecclesiastical institutions, but their history is that of man in the world. This history has been restored, as it were, to contemporary men, due largely to the work of Étienne Gilson and his collaborators at the Pontifical Institute of Mediaeval Studies and to Stephan Kuttner and the Institute of Research and Study in Medieval Canon Law. Although the scientific study of medieval philosophy began at Louvain and the scientific study of canon law began within the German and Austrian empires, the entry of these subjects into the work of historians was effected by Gilson and Kuttner. By their exact and laborious penetration of the original sources, the face of philosophy and the face of law at the beginning of our Western European civilization have become evident. Without their work it was impossible to write a true account of the intellectual life of our civilization. They have enlarged the self-awareness of the Church, but also the consciousness of humanity. Again, the successful formula appears to be dedicated genius, a few collaborators, a small corporate form.

Financial support has also been a necessity. In Lagrange's case it came from the Dominican order; in the case of the Institute of Medieval Studies it has come from the Basilian Congregation; in the case of the Institute of Canon Law it has come from individuals including individual bishops, the Fritz Thyssen Stiftung and the government of the United States. In each case the formation of a library has accompanied the work of scholarship, but a library not viewed as a dead depository of dead materials, but as a collection alive through its use by specialists. In each case books and money have been at the service of a guiding spirit.

A critic might observe, "None of your instances show Catholic scholarship serving the great needs of humanity for peace, freedom, and domestic life." I must confess the belief that research is distinct from political action. If that distinction is observed, these great needs of the human community will not be met by scholarly research. The work of scholars is a contribution to, in Maritain's phrase, the supratemporal common good.[5] Yet if such work must be justified in pragmatic political terms, it is evident that an increase in awareness of one's identity, purposes, and potentialities affords both a better sense of the essential and a wider range of options for action; and through the efforts of the scholars this sense and this range become the shared good of the community.

That research is not an end in itself isolated from the rest of Christian life needs no doubt to be said. I have mentioned the imperfect integration of biblical studies. In all branches of academic activity, there is the danger of mandarinism, which may be defined here as the self-contained search for perfection within a discipline without regard to human utility. As perfection is not possible here below, so refinement

[5]Jacques Maritain, *The Person and the Common Good* (trans. John J. Fitzgerald 1947, University of Notre Dame Press, 1967) p. 61.

and super-refinement are always possible. The assiduous editor of texts will suppose that one more variant of a commonplace conjunction will in some realm of perfect texts make a difference. Disciples will labor to add unnecessary glosses to what has been in substance done. If those within academe do not have the sense to direct their energies elsewhere, it is right and proper that an outside body should say, "These are now our needs." It is the advantage of Catholic scholars that their exists for them such a benevolent body as the bishops to call them from absorption in reverie or overrefinement.

The kind of specialized institute I am describing in terms of Lagrange, Gilson, and Kuttner could be adequately funded with an endowment of $5,000,000—enough to pay the salaries of a senior scholar or two, a visiting scholar or two, junior collaborators and secretaries, and also to pay for the acquisition of books, journals, microfilms, and manuscripts. Let us imagine a scholar or small number of scholars stirred by the Church's appeal so that they renounce the self-satisfaction of mandarinism even as they eschew the tangible recognition attendant on specific problem-solving. He, or she, or they, seek to engage in research in depth, so that what has often been a curse of Catholic educators, the belief that solutions exist, ready-made, in the authorities, holds no temptation for them. Not for them to solve economic problems by invoking the words of the Lord, "Lend freely hoping nothing thereby" (Luke 6:35); not for them to solve ecclesiastical problems by the example in scripture of Paul's handing over the sinner of Corinth (1 Cor. 5:5); not for them to answer sexual problems by drawing on the wisdom of the Fathers and invoking Augustine's insistence that procreative purpose alone justifies marital intercourse; not for them to see the structure of marriage forever determined by the pronouncements of the Council of Trent and its requirement of the parish priest or delegate for the validity of the sacrament of marriage; not for them to resolve issues of modern life by translating the latest papal encyclical. In none of these authoritative sources do they suppose that answers can be found which can be transposed to problem areas without the most careful examination of the areas and determination of the relation between the authoritative answer and the problem now confronted. They know by heart the lesson that when the question changes the answer cannot be the same.

Let us suppose they also resist that opposite temptation, so often understandably succumbed to by American Catholic institutions, of copying blindly a secular form. Not for them, for example, to reproduce the Kinsey Institute of Sex Research. They have before them for imitation a Lagrange, a Gilson, or a Kuttner, and their institutes. They have what are distinct assets of Catholic culture in the American environment—a belief that theory is important, in contrast to a prevailing pragmatism; a sense of international community and historical inheritance, in contrast to the technocratic impulse to let techniques determine the human good. Suppose these imaginary scholars, who have the best of Catholic attainments and who have avoided the faults scholars are prone to, setting out to study the structures of the Church or the structures of the family. What specifically shall we ask of them?

Unquestionably, in studying the structure of the Church, we should ask its student to be master of a large body of biblical and theological literature, of canon law, of intellectual and institutional history, of the biographies of a variety of saints, doctors, and popes; and in addition to all this matter coming from the life of the Church, we should expect a certain sophistication in one or more of such modern academic disciplines as anthropology, economics, law, political science, or sociology. We should expect a fusion of religious insights, theological tradition, historical data, and modern methodology, yielding new and richer ways of seeing the Church. *A pari*, we should expect of the scholar investigating the family a comparable mastery of biblical, theological, and canonical literature and knowledge of the apposite intellectual and institutional history. The experience of the Church in shaping the conditions under which sexuality is made purposeful, the education of children is undertaken, and human love is expressed is complex. Who unaware of it can write of the Christian family? The ecclesial symbolism of marriage can scarcely be ignored. Our scholar is dealing with an institution shaped by religion, law, convention, and instincts, analyzed by demographers, economists, lawyers, psychologists, social biologists, and sociologists, and celebrated in all literatures. A knowledge of one or more of those literatures and one or more of those modern disciplines is indispensable. A knowledge of languages is presupposed.

I set out of course the ideal, towards which our scholars will strive. Sometimes, observing what is realized, I wonder if anyone who has not received a classical European education will approximate it. Certainly, to the extent that any college or university insists on narrow disciplinary bounds for its students and demands many hours of classroom instruction from its faculty, it impedes the realization of the ideal. It does so equally if its requirements of students become so flabby that the time when intellectual development should be strenuous becomes a period of unfocused dabbling. If among all our Catholic colleges we could have one *école normale* with the most rigorous academic standards applicable to all, that Catholic college would contribute immensely to the advancement of our ideal.

Should we ask more of our scholars than the interdisciplinary mastery I have outlined? We copy the secularist liberals, I suggest, if we believe that the character and motivation of the scholar are irrelevant to the scholarly enterprise, and these are the secular liberals of the Enlightenment whose symbols, as Archbishop Bernardin suggested, are dying with their dying culture, on which Marxism is a revenge. We share with the Marxists our international outlook, a sense of history, a trust in theory, and moral convictions about the seriousness of human endeavor. Shall we be Marxists, too? What they neglect is the importance of the individual human heart. Its centrality is our heritage and our most cherished conviction. We can, therefore, say that in scholarship courage and candor are as necessary as ingenuity of technique and agility of mind. The love of God and neighbor are not substitutes for wisdom, but is wisdom present in a heart where love has been doubted or turned inward?

In neither case would the scholars of the Church or the family seek, qua scholars, to make their findings or their synthesis into new norms for action in the Church. They would seek an interested audience, unprepared as every audience is for new perspectives. If their work was to bear fruit, they would need assistance. Here the universities, the learned societies, and the bishops would have a role. A mixed commission of bishops and academics would be helpful to mediate their work to the larger community. If the transfusion of their ideas into the mainstream of the Church were to be complete, bishops would be chosen from their number, as in the twelfth century the masters of the new canonical lore of Bologna became shapers of the Church, as in our time Cardinal Bea moved from biblical studies to ecumenical leadership and the sees of Winnipeg and Toronto have been filled by participants in the Pontifical Institute of Medieval Studies. Such mediation to the community through personal apprehension of ideas is important. Yet if the ideas developed by sound research have power, they will be received by the community. To adapt a phrase of Learned Hand, "Power and the exercise of power must needs coalesce."

So far, as you have observed, my models and imaginary instances have all involved the use of professedly Christian matter, integrated with new data and approaches. A neutral observer might say, "You have spoken of scriptural studies, medieval philosophy, canon law, ecclesiology, and Christian family morality? Can you offer no examples of scholarship other than of Christians reconstructing the thought of earlier Christians? Granted that what Christians think and do is part of the human good, why do you not consider directly what scholarship could do in aid of the Church's service to those outside the community of believers?'' I can only speak of what I know, so I shall speak of what might be done in law. Perhaps, with appropriate modifications, what I say of law could be paralleled in other fields. As you will observe, I shift now from looking at pure research to research bearing fruit in teaching and public service.

There are worldwide some forty pontifical universities with faculties of law or canon law; there are twenty-three American Catholic universities with law schools; there are over a hundred American seminaries with professors of canon law. The tradition of Catholic legal scholarship is the oldest in the Western world, reaching back to Bologna "the mother of law schools,'' where in the twelfth century law teachers, termed *magistri*, and small groups of students, termed *socii* or associates of the teacher, set out on the magnificent enterprise of bringing reason into the rules of Church and society. The teachers of Bologna knew the power of the hypothetical to instruct, the necessity of reference to case decisions, and the importance of dialectically developing rational rules. They took from their imperial Roman model a rule-oriented and rule-bound understanding of what law consisted in, and they looked for reason as often in authorities as in human needs. None of their modern descendants, it seems fair to say, have had a substantial impact on modern legal education.

The three major innovations—the casebook instead of the legal treatise, the oral classroom dialectic instead of the lecture, the student-edited law review instead of the learned journal—were made at Harvard Law School in the last part of the nineteenth century. Bologna and the Church did not contribute to them. The methods and also the assumptions dominant in this country came from the much younger institution in Cambridge, Massachusetts, and these methods and assumptions have permeated every law school, whatever its religious affiliation, within the United States. Such moves as Notre Dame's in sponsoring a journal of legal theory edited by adults, or, for a period of years, making Professional Responsibility a mandatory first-year course, have been individual gestures in an academic world dominated by Langdell's view of law as a science, by Pound's metaphor of social engineering, by Holmes's attempted separation of law and morals, and by a pervasive professional pragmatism. If the success of the methodology and outlook may be explained in part by their congruence with the desires of the dominant social class, should not the Christian law schools carry the responsibility for offering no alternative? Were not the faculties of canon law more static in their devotion to rules than the secular faculties who grasped the dynamism of the equally rulebound approach of Langdell, Pound, and Holmes? Did not the law schools of the American Catholic universities at least benefit from the legal realists' view that law is a process? Yet could we not now as Christians design a law school more sensitive to the needs of society and the aspirations of the individual person?

I believe we could and here make bold to say what might be done. The starting point is that law is a process—the insight of the legal realists which we must appropriate as Lagrange appropriated the methods of agnostic biblical criticism. But we must add that not only is a law a process—it is a process in which the actors are persons, interacting in terms of rules. To understand the process requires comprehension of the persons as much as of the rules. This perspective requires a shift in the matter of law curricula, which are now composed almost entirely of the opinions of appellate courts and the texts of statutes, supplemented by the analysis of such opinions and statutes in treatises and articles. It requires a substantial infusion of biography, as the lives of the lawyers, judges, and litigants are seen as part of the legal process to be comprehended. The impersonal legal world of A and B, which Bologna knew too, must be complemented by an examination of the individual circumstances in which persons are given or denied compensation, set free or sent to prison, held to their bargains or released from their bonds. Literature and drama must be recognized as legitimate means of comprehending legal issues; but legal history, understood comprehensively as the study of the process and the persons in it, must share with old-fashioned case analysis the burden of instruction.

Further, it might be acknowledged that theory as to the purposes of man is essential to the shaping of law. Jurisprudence would no longer be an elective luxury but the study of the philosophy of law and the philosophy of man would be formally pursued in each year of legal education. In a Catholic law school, theory would embrace theology as well as philosophy.

Finally, the responsibilities of lawyers might be articulated as a matter of individual conscience and social expectations. These responsibilities would not be studied in the minimalist terms of a professional code—such code-directed morality becomes a course in line-drawing and evasion. The students would be invited to look at situations in which lawyers have actually acted, to ask themselves if as human persons they would want to act in this fashion, to ask what structural changes in the legal system are desirable to encourage lawyers to act as persons and to help others in the process as persons. Law schools, no more than any other school, cannot assure that their graduates will behave morally. But they can examine and criticize the conditions for morality in the profession. They can assure that students are aware that there is a moral aspect to their professional actions, and by text and example they can convey what is personally and socially expected of lawyers. They can destroy at the roots the notion that a lawyer's role suppresses his humanity and that the profession of law is the performance of a technical service.

If these changes were carried out in but one law school of high academic standards, if they were not blunted by the compromises of faculties and diluted by academic bureaucracy, other schools would follow; and the model set by a Catholic law school here could be followed not only by American schools of civil law but by faculties of canon law, and by universities abroad as well as at home. The changes would affect that process by which peace is kept and goods distributed in our society. Would not the providing of such a model wherein lawyers became oriented to persons be a substantial service of scholarship to that humanity we as Christians are called to serve?

I have been asked to pose the academic issues involved in the cooperation of scholars with the Church. In retrospect, you may see what I have thought them to be: Is collaboration to be by survey, poll, and consultations? Are all the Catholic colleges and seminaries to play a part? What are the best models for research? Is a Catholic Rand desirable? Should we concentrate on a Catholic Institute of Advanced Studies or a Catholic Center of rotating Fellows? What kind of qualifications should the research scholars have? How would the findings and syntheses of researchers in depth be appropriated by the larger community? What would be an instance of a Christian perspective affecting a discipline serving the world at large? You have my answers as well as the questions implicitly asked. Mine are: Concentrate resources. Have a *normalien* school of excellence at, at least, one Catholic college. Develop one or at the most two research institutes in the great problem areas. Reshape the thinking of our professional schools by a personalism rooted in that community of love of the Lord in which we are sharers. You may have different answers.

Eucharistic Liturgy:
Homily
Most Rev. William D. Borders

The gospel of today's Mass is certainly apropos for a liturgy wherein we join together in community in miniature, hopefully representing a mission of evangelization proper to colleges and universities. Christ in the gospel today invites Peter and Andrew, James and John, to make a vital step of commitment and follow him. Theirs was to be a mission charged to implement the teaching of Christ; called generously to share in his love that, if accepted, could change the world. Furthermore, we who are associated with Catholic universities and colleges, even though committed to highly specialized disciplines, must share in the commitment of the apostles. For this reason we also share in the work of the Church, and our ultimate mission is the same. The mission of the Church takes different forms; it is expressed in different ecclesiologies, developed within the halls of learning, proclaimed in union halls, in the political arena, and in economic thrusts and counterthrusts. This is true because Christ came to invite all men to share his kingdom, and no person or activity is separate and apart from his creative and redemptive love.

One of our position papers referred to John Henry Newman, who wrote of the university more than 100 years ago and succinctly described the university in relationship to the totality of the formation of the man—and I quote:

> It will not satisfy me, what satisfies too many, to have two independent systems, at once, side by side, but sort of a division of labor, and only accidentally brought together.... I want the same roof to contain both the intellectual and moral disciplines; devotion is not a sort of finish given to the sciences; nor is science a sort of feather in the cap, if I

may so express myself, an ornament and set-off to devotion. I want the intellectual layman to be religious, and devout ecclesiastics to be intellectual.

Will you excuse me if I refer to a similar modern orientation at home. Within the archdiocese of Baltimore we tried to express, during a period of nine months, the mission of the archdiocese, stating the mission of the Church for our particular time of history within our diverse cultures, and hopefully creating an atmosphere wherein a people can grow in union with each other, truly creating a faith community. We thought it necessary to understand our mission before establishing priorities and further develop programs.

I will quote only the Preamble to our Mission Statement:

> We, the Church in the Archdiocese of Baltimore, are a community of Catholic Christians who are gathered by the Holy Spirit to recognize in the person of Jesus, in His life and teaching, in His dying and rising, the expression of the Father's freely given and continual love of all people, and to live out, as individuals and as a community, our commitment to Jesus and to His mission: to proclaim and teach, to express and model, and to advocate and serve the Kingdom of God as the Spirit brings it to reality in the whole of God's creation, more particularly within the hearts of loving people.
>
> Therefore, our mission as a Church is to proclaim, in our words and in our actions, in our teaching and public life; to express and model in our Eucharistic gatherings and life as a community; and to serve in our complete dedication to all people the becoming of the Kingdom of God, which is a wider and deeper reality than the Church itself.

In the same manner, the Catholic college and university must have a unique position within the mission of the Church. We are facing up to this by titling our symposium "Evangelization in the American Context." Martin Marty offers us a working definition: "To evangelize," he states, "means to meet people in situations where the gospel of Jesus Christ is given the opportunity to change individuals and groups and to bring them towards wholeness." Bishop Law this morning, in quoting the Holy Father, developed the concept within scriptural context: "Evangelization is the grace and mission proper to the Church. . . . The good news is meant for all people at all times."

If we are to accept a challenge in our own times, we must be possessed of the necessary resources. The most fundamental of all would be that we are a community of faith. We cannot proclaim that which we do not possess in love. Yet we must be a particular kind of faith community, for our mission exists in the future even more than it exists in the present. We have resources to challenge thought; correlate the eternal truths revealed by Christ with the increasing knowledge we have of God's creation. We must know where we are and also must live with an ecclesiology that can relate to the world in which we live.

Father Avery Dulles, in his excellent book *Models of the Church*, presents various possible models. He indicates that any one model is incomplete and therefore necessarily includes aspects of other models, but nonetheless the dominant one will be effective in a particular place, time, and culture. You will remember these models as: Institution, Mystical Communion, Sacrament, Herald, and Servant.

In order to illustrate how the college or university as a faith community can accomplish its mission, I would like to use one of these models as an example. In the opening paragraph of *Lumen Gentium*, the Church was described "as a Sacrament or sign"; again in paragraph 48 the Church is described as "the universal Sacrament of salvation." While this concept might have seemed new a few years ago, it certainly was not and is not a new reality. From apostolic times the Church accomplished her mission only when witness to Christ was made manifest in the lives of Christians. "By this men will know that you are my disciples if you have love one for another."

However, within the limitations of our individual and corporate lives we did not always advert to this fundamental reality. We who were of the preconciliar Church seemed to have viewed ourselves as an institution, as a kind of sanctuary of salvation. Most of us would consider a sanctuary as a place of refuge situated in a hostile environment. We justified our existence by bringing people within our protective atmosphere and nourishing them. Possibly the same attitudes existed within many of our colleges and universities. Because of this orientation we did not adequately influence the culture, values, ideals, and morals of our country in a manner in which our heritage demands.

May I borrow from a Maryknoll priest, Father William Frazier, who comments on the juxtaposition of sanctuary and sign:

> Unlike a sanctuary, a sign is meant to point beyond itself and to have its import outside itself. Unlike a sanctuary, a sign is not an enclosure, but a disclosure. A sign performs its function not by containing but by communicating; not by annexation but by representation. In relation to their respective environments, sign is a humble image, sanctuary a haughty one; sign is an image of service, sanctuary an image of separation; a sign is cooperative, a sanctuary competitive; a sanctuary finds within itself any action which is really important, a sign points beyond itself where the action is. In a word, the main improvement of sign over sanctuary as an image or model of the Church is the quality of openness to its environment which in application to the Church means openness to the world.

The Catholic college and university must have this openness to the world, accepting so much that is wonderful and good, but offering to the world the revelation received from Christ. Christians have not been called to the Church for their own sake, but for the sake of others—to serve as a sign and instrument of God's universal saving purpose.

I hope that we of the academic community accept our role as instruments of God during this period of salvation history. We surely do not need to take a defensive stance. We do not know the future, nor do we need to have such knowledge. We do know, however, that we have a mission. Our mission within the Church is certainly not coextensive with the mission of God; the mission of God is the all-embracing power of salvation always and everywhere, whereas the mission of the Church has its own special role to play within the broader process. The mission of the university and college also has a special role; this must include being a witness—a sign of salvation that reaches the roots of every human situation.

Our possibilities are not fully recognized and are without known limits, for we are living and working within the mystery of God's providence shared in the redemptive love of Jesus Christ. If we grow in depth both on the level of knowledge and love we will have the capacity to reach out beyond our own boundaries and make a broader contribution by penetrating the thought of the total educational community and thus the world in which we live.

III. PANELS
January 13

Projecting the Immediate Future:
1. *Ways and Means*
Most Rev. William E. McManus

How can a bishop help a Catholic university or college in his diocese advance evangelization in the American context?

I will propose six ways in order of priority: (1) include the university or college in a diocesan pastoral plan of evangelization; (2) be involved directly in its designation or description of its Catholic identity; (3) frequently and consistently authenticate and commend its evangelical commitments and accomplishments; (4) zealously recruit students; (5) center diocesan programs of continuing education in the university or college; (6) collaborate with fund-raising endeavors.

Later I will suggest some ways for university and college presidents to help a bishop with his diocesan plan for evangelization.

At the end of this talk I will make a few remarks about an inquiry which Rome's Sacred Congregation on Catholic Education has addressed to bishops and to university and college presidents.

The proceedings this morning will conclude with a free-for-all discussion.

I

Include the Catholic University or College in a Diocesan Plan of Evangelization.

Lest I exasperate my brother bishops by exhorting them at this early morning hour I will deal with this point mainly in a personal way. This will present little difficulty because my diocese is a place called Mesarfelta, distinguished in church lore because of much uncertainty about its whereabouts. So I can speak freely without disturbing the folks at home.

Somewhat like a student immersed in a Berlitz intensive, crash-style course in a language I recently saturated my mind with information and commentary on evangelization. Like a Berlitz graduate, I can speak the language but I still don't know much about evangelization in depth. This much, however, I now do know. I need a much more personal and a much more deeply interiorized theology of evangelization. Without it I will not be able to measure up fully to the Church's expectations of me, expectations set forth in detail in the Vatican Directory on the Pastoral Ministry of Bishops and in the Holy Father's recent Apostolic Exhortation on Evangelization. With a personal theology of evangelization well thought out in my mind and embraced in my heart I may be able to exercise the kind of leadership sincerely desired of me by many, including, I think, the Catholic university and college community.

In his Apostolic Exhortation on Evangelization Pope Paul VI refers to Jesus Christ as "the very first and greatest evangelizer." Describing Jesus' evangelization the pope says, "Going from town to town, preaching to the poorest—and frequently the most receptive—the joyful news of the fulfillment of the promises and of the covenant offered by God is the mission for which Jesus declares that he is sent by the Father. And all aspects of his mystery—the incarnation itself, his miracles, his teaching, the gathering together of the disciples, the sending out of the Twelve, the cross and the resurrection, the permanence of his presence in the midst of his own— were components of his evangelizing activity."

"To evangelize: what meaning did this imperative have for Christ?", the pope asks. "It certainly is not easy," he says, "to express in a complete synthesis the meaning, the content, and the modes of evangelization as Jesus conceived it and put it into practice. In any case, the attempt to make such a synthesis will never end."

Indeed, an endless problem in Jesus' public life were two simultaneous calls: one from his Father to preach the eternal truths of revelation and the other from his brethren to minister to the human needs. At times this problem became so perplexing that Jesus wanted to flee from it. Don't say anything more about my miracles, he once said to his disciples, and on another occasion he put out to sea for an unannounced destination to get away from an overly-enthusiastic crowd which wanted to reward him for his miracles by making him their king. During his get-away-from-it-all retreats in the desert and during the quiet night hours on Lake Galilee with his fisherman friends, Jesus probably pondered the very same question confronting today's evangelist, viz., how much time to devote to preaching and how much to ministry?

That's my problem—how to divide my time, my life, between preaching and ministry. There is no easy answer, like saying that both are equally important and I'll do my best at each. Such vagueness would leave me prey to impulses and reactions and could lead to flighty indulgence in spiritual sprees and in scratching away at various apostolic itches. On my knees in prayer with the Holy Spirit I have to work out a personal answer based on the teaching and example of Jesus Christ, Church doctrine on the episcopacy and evangelization, the signs of the times, and a full appraisal of my talents, limitations and energies. At peace with myself I would feel calm and confident in going to work on a diocesan pastoral plan for evangelization.

Approaching this task I would recall Pope Paul's succinct observation that Vatican II's many objectives are "definitively summed up in this single one: to make the Church of the twentieth century ever better fitted for proclaiming the gospel to the people of the twentieth century." To set up a preliminary agenda for my diocesan plan of evangelization I would turn to the Holy Father's summation of the Bishops' World Synod on Evangelization in 1974. "Fidelity both to a message whose servants we are and to the people to whom we must transmit it living and intact is," the pope says, "the central axis of evangelization." It poses three burning questions which the 1974 Synod kept constantly in mind:

(1) In our day, what has happened to the hidden energy of the Good News which is able to have a powerful effect on man's conscience?

(2) To what extent and in what way is that evangelical force capable of really transforming the people of this century?

(3) What methods should be followed in order that the power of the gospel may have its effect?

For help in developing in-depth answers to these profound questions I would go to the Catholic university or college in my diocese with an invitation phrased in Pope Paul's forthright declaration: "Men of learning—whether you be theologians, exegetes or historians—the work of evangelization needs your tireless work of research and your care and tact in transmitting the truth to which your studies lead you." If my invitation were accepted, I would organize a Council of University and College Scholars to assist the diocese with its plans and programs for evangelization and to help me personally with my leadership role in this endeavor.

At the risk of sounding idealistically naive I now will project my view of a two-year agenda for a Diocesan Council of Scholars.

Theology and Religious Studies: A declaration of doctrinal premises for the diocese's pastoral plan of evangelization. This declaration, solidly based on sound doctrine, is to be phrased in understandable, appealing, and contemporary language with its message aimed directly at the people of the diocese.

Philosophy and Psychology: A report on the predominant processes and patterns of thinking in various intellectual strata in the diocese. How can the diocese's evangelizers best make contact with the modern mind?

Social Studies and Sociology: A survey of Church membership and an analysis of the reasons for diminishing association with the institutional Church. Identification and description of the areas of society in the diocese for which the Church has a compelling obligation to minister to human needs. Proposed priorities in the diocese's social apostolate.

Communication Arts and Skills: Formation of a committee to edit the bishop's pastoral communications for maximum effectiveness. Organization of a liturgical laboratory to make use of contemporary music and art forms in liturgical celebrations. In-service education for preachers, lectors, bulletin editors, and others engaged in communication activities.

Inter-Disciplinary Dialogue: Are the Diocesan Council's theologians and philosophers both speaking the same language of evangelization? Are the Church's doctrines as phrased by the theologians and philosophers communicable to the people?

Pastoral Services: Ministry on the campus; ministry to commuter students; ministry to the faculty.

Obviously this is an incomplete agenda, and its recital may have irritated historians, anthropologists, and other scholars who feel their wisdom also would be useful for evangelization. Let the agenda rest as an unfinished example of a good idea.

Departing from this first point I leave this final thought. A highly effective way for a diocese to evangelize a university or college is to involve it in evangelizing the diocese.

II

Be Involved Directly in a University's or College's Designation or Description of Its Catholic Identity.

"Bishop, is that university or college in your diocese *still* Catholic?" This is a favorite rhetorical question sometimes used by persons who have made up their minds that the institution no longer is Catholic and want the bishop to confirm their opinion. If he dares to answer affirmatively, he'll be acused of not being Catholic himself. If he appears to duck the question by saying truthfully that he is not informed about the institution's inner affairs, he is going to limp away from the conversation after being badly bruised by invectives about his failure to protect the faith of the young in his diocese.

Not all questions on this matter are loaded. Increasingly priests and laity are addressing to their bishops sincerely open-minded questions about a particular institution's Catholicity. These questions often are prompted by startling announcements, e.g., the college now is a private, nonsectarian institution; a board of trustees and not the religious order now has full control of the college's properties and programs; an undergraduate course in biblical criticism will be taught by a Lutheran minister; the pros and cons of the abortion issue will be debated at a public meeting on campus; a survey showing that less than a third of the Catholics living on campus regularly go to Sunday Mass.

Some bishops admit to being in the dark about the Catholic posture and policies of institutions of higher learning in their own dioceses and to knowing little about present trends in American Catholic higher education. Though some bishops are perplexed by allegations and rumors about things less than truly Catholic in a university or college they hesitate to take any action for fear that it might be interpreted as a lack of trust in the judgment and good will of the university or college authorities. Meanwhile the authorities become more and more suspicious and fearful that one of these days the bishop may be denouncing them.

The time has come to call a halt to this shadow boxing. Bishops and university and college authorities should get together for a clear understanding of the institution's definition and description of its Catholicity. Beyond this understanding, the bishop should participate in the institution's on-going efforts to clarify its claim to the title Catholic.

In a brilliant essay on interaction between university and Church, an essay from which I probably am not the only borrower at this meeting, Father Ladislas Orsy, S.J., observes:

> How to be Catholic? Let us stress the need for raising this question because, for some universities with a strong Catholic past, the danger is *drifting*. Drifting means a lack of courage or capacity to assess with clarity the state of the university and to plan on the basis of facts the future interplay between the university and the Christian community. Some universities have the means for building up an overall Christian orientation; others have the capacity to accept a restricted presence of Christianity. But there may be universities or colleges that do not have the means to build or the capacity to accept a Christian dimension. For them the question is how to move intelligently in the direction of a fully secular university that by the signs of the times it should become. Because nothing human is alien to the Church, such universities need not consider their course as defection from the Catholic cause but as the embracing of human values that the Church ought to respect.

As Father Orsy says in his essay, the main question to be raised in a discussion of an institution's Catholicity is not whether it is in essence a Catholic institution nor whether it has added some Catholic dimensions to its secular program nor whether it has a legal charter from the Church nor whether it has Catholic services on campus. The main question is: "What is this Catholic university or college *doing* to be Catholic truthfully?"

Truthfulness, according to Father Orsy, requires that all nominal solutions should be rejected. Legal charters from the Church may serve a good purpose but they cannot give Christian life to a university. Neither can a claim for Catholicity on the part of the administration create a religious option when in reality it is not there.

Let me briefly mention Father Orsy's signs of true Catholicism in a university or college.

(1) The academic community's free choice (a) "to bring the sacred and the transcendental, in the form of Christianity, into the life of the university and make it operative there" and (b) to enter into a university-Church community, a visible community of mutual respect and support.

59

(2) The university's or college's ongoing, repeatedly proclaimed, completely truthful commitment to the sacred and the transcendental, in the form of Christianity, in the life of the institution, and its unequivocal, institutional commitment to a communion with the Church in a spirit of mutual respect and support.

(3) A spirit of creativity designed to reinforce and to expand the academic community's and the institution's commitment to the sacred and to the Church.

A truly Catholic university or college is not decreed; it is created. In this noble work of creation the bishop has a vital role to play.

III

Frequently and Consistently Authenticate and Commend the University's or College's Evangelical Commitments and Accomplishments.

In the Vatican's Directory on the Pastoral Ministry of Bishops there is an especially interesting chapter entitled: *How To Exercise Episcopal Authority.* One paragraph is so applicable to this point that it merits quotation in full.

> While exercising authority in the service of the faithful who form a community of faith and love, the bishop is careful to respect their legitimate liberty to think differently. In various questions he does his best to consult everybody concerned, and, for his part, as far as justice and charity permit, he does not withhold full and accurate information from those who ask for it. He fosters discussions among the faithful of different conditions and different ages, but the principle is to be kept clear that, when it comes to determining programs of pastoral action and ways to accomplish them the decision—after suggestions have been heard and examined— belongs to the bishop who, according to the seriousness of the matter and his own prudent judgment, will make the decision alone or collegially.

In short, a bishop is to be open-minded, candid, and decisive. These characteristics should assure him a warm welcome on a university or college campus where open-mindedness and candor are traits highly esteemed in an authentic leader. Where a bishop can be both comfortable and influential is where he ought to be as much as possible. By going out of his way to authenticate, often by his presence alone, and to commend a university or college project of evangelization, a bishop may develop a rapport with the academic community which is meritorious in itself and may also serve the useful purpose of discouraging illegal or irresponsible activities deserving of the bishop's censure or objection.

Authenticating the good can be far more effective pastorally than condemning evil.

IV

Zealously Recruit Students.

To presume that thousands of high school graduates will continue indefinitely to drift into Catholic universities and colleges as they have for the past 25 years is to ignore the ominous data on the steadily declining enrollment in elementary and secondary schools and the nation's downward birth rate. By 1980 at the latest Catholic universities and colleges will be in a tightly competitive market for students. Already hard-pressed to make financial ends meet with all space occupied, our institutions of higher education may not be able to continue with substantially reduced enrollment.

Let's open all the doors to college recruiters, e.g., Catholic high schools, CCD high school instruction classes, pastoral letters, the diocesan paper, parish pulpits, radio and TV spots, advertising, etc. A bishop's zeal could spark this activity in his diocese. No small fringe benefit from this effort will be publicity on the diocese's endorsement of the importance and value of Catholic higher education in the work of evangelization.

V

Center Diocesan Programs of Continuing Education in the Catholic University or College.

A university's or college's survival and an outstanding service to the diocese can be linked in a diocesan sponsored program of continuing education for clergy, religious and laity. As I have said a few moments ago, our universities and colleges are going to need students, full-time, part-time, "any-time." Survival depends upon the life blood of enrollment. A diocese needs up-dated education for clergy and laity upon whom it depends for its programs of evangelization.

A university's or college's Catholicity will be enhanced by the on-campus presence of adults in quest of more education to help them fulfill their evangelical responsibilities in the diocese. By the same token, the diocese will gain from higher education services otherwise not available to it. Evangelization will be the principal beneficiary of this arrangement.

VI

Collaborate with Fund-Raising Endeavors.

Because money is a decidedly specific reality I will not bore you with glittering generalities about it. Suffice it to say that a bishop's positive attitude toward a college or univeristy can be significantly influential in attracting bequests and other substantial donations. To generate this positive attitude a university or college should not hesitate to lay out its financial condition before the bishop, but not with the ulterior motive of trying to persuade him immediately to order special collections. At most, I would think, a university or college should expect a bishop to be an active collaborator with its own fund-raising venture.

Much earlier in this paper I said I would suggest some ways for a university or college president to help a bishop with his diocesan plan for evangelization. Without reneging, I am going to be brief on this point lest the length of this paper intrude into the time on the program for discussion.

First and foremost, I propose that a president favorably respond to the initiatives which I have recommended to a bishop and that in the absence of such initiative by the bishop the president try to get things started along the lines I have suggested in this paper.

Open *all* the doors to let the bishop into even the back rooms from which, perhaps for his own good, he has been excluded.

Be generous in giving the bishop sound advice on pastoral matters and help him be an authentic and appealing leader in the diocese and in the academic community.

Remember that a bishop is not a potted palm to be added to the scenery at a commencement or convocation. By tradition and by mandate of the Church he is, as a successor of the apostles, duty bound to teach the word of God with authority and bear witness to it, faithfully to guard it, and authentically to interpret it.

In a large archdiocese or diocese, be willing to accept a priest as the delegated representative of the bishop provided the priest can give evidence of his close contact with his bishop and assurance of the bishop's full support of his activities.

Forty years ago at the University of Saint Mary of the Lake in Mundelein, Illinois, my semester exam in canon law asked in Latin: "What is the earliest hour at which a priest in Nome, Alaska, using one of the canonical options for telling time, may begin anticipation of the divine office *juxta suum horologium?*" Preoccupied with trying to recall Nome's latitude and longitude which had something to do with canon law's time-telling process I inadvertently and stupidly translated *juxta suum horologium* into "according to my watch" instead of according to *his* watch. My answer was off the mark by about half a day. My professor, the eminent Father T. Lincoln Bouscaren, circulated mimeographed copies of my answer among the seminary's faculty and students as an outstanding illustration of "not getting the state of the question." Though the canonical times in Nome still are unknown to me, getting the state of the question has become one of my better habits.

During the past week I tried hard to get the state of the question in recent inquiries from the Congregation on Catholic Education to bishops and the chief administrative officers of Catholic universities, colleges, and seminaries. This attempt included a review of the official documentation, conversations with several persons who have been preparing replies to the Congregation's questions, and a search for perspective within which to see the present inquiry. Most lacking in my present understanding is perspective, the big picture developed internationally during the past ten years of interaction between the Congregation and the universities. At this time I am unable to react responsibly to proposed refinements of norms which in their unrefined condition I have not fully comprehended.

Lacking a firm grasp on the state of the question I am unwilling to risk any response to it beyond a report to you that at its meeting in Washington last week the USCC Committee on Education authorized its chairman and the Education Department's staff to synthesize the contents of letters which Archbishop Borders has received from some of the

Ordinaries of archdioceses and dioceses where Catholic universities and colleges are located. These letters contain indirect replies to some of the questions raised by the Congregation and both some general and specific comments on the relationship of the Ordinary and the Catholic institutions of higher education.

The USCC Committee on Education also recommended that one of the forum sessions during the NCCB-USCC May 1976 meeting be on the topic of Catholic higher education in the United States. A panel representative of several and divergent points of view will be invited to address the bishops attending the forum. This recommendation has been put on the agenda for the USCC Administrative Board meeting in February.

On this last point of my talk I can say no more formally other than to promise a continuation of my homework on Catholic higher education.

Projecting the Immediate Future:
2. *Ways and Means*
Barbara Thomas, S.C.N.

When I was invited to speak on this topic, I was somewhat ambivalent about accepting the invitation, noting that the participants were to be members of the hierarchy, administrators of universities and colleges, scholars and specialists; and that the symposium was designed to explore collaboration between Catholic colleges and universities in the wider Catholic community under the generic rubric of research. However, after some reflection on the purpose of the meeting and the reason for my being asked, which seemed to be to share my experience of the university and Catholic college as a major superior of women, I accepted the invitation and prepared for this session by engaging in conversation with some of our own sisters and with sisters across the United States who either have served or are presently serving in colleges and universities. I speak to you directly out of my experience as a leader of women religious.

I would like to do this by reflecting on the relationship between the religious congregation of women and the educational institutions of higher learning. I will refer to this relationship as mission, as the religious mission. I would also like to reflect briefly on the changing shape of the mission of the women religious in the Church, and lastly on the promise of complementarity between this religious mission and Catholic universities and colleges throughout our country. I stand before you as one who is very much interested in continued presence of women religious in Catholic universities and colleges. In order to explore the possibility of this continued presence, I feel that I must explore the role of the university and college in light of their ability to live out the mission of the religious congregation, necessarily the broader mission of the Church. Whenever I use the word *mission*, even though I use it specifically in reference to the religious congregation of women, I am specifically talking about the mission of the Church.

I realize that I do not have the whole picture, I do not stand in the shoes of the presidents and others who share the administration of our educational institutions. I do not share directly the experience of our faculties nor of our students. But as a superior of women religious who is in conversation with other women, women in my own community and other communities across our country, as the moderator of a corporation board, as one who is continually dealing with sponsoring groups and with individuals who are or who are not motivated to continue to serve in our educational institutions, I believe that I do reflect the experience of an important segment of the Church's life in our country. Given our purpose for being here together and having the opportunity to reflect on the role, nature, and mission of the Catholic university or college, I ask you to reflect with me at this time in an effort to share responsibility for moving toward any change that may be necessary for the life of our colleges and universities in the future.

Some questions might help us focus the issue. Why is it that in this year of 1976 there are many alert, intelligent, some young and some not so young, women religious who find it difficult either to move toward or to maintain their service in educational institutions of higher learning? Why is it that these same women do not experience themselves as ministers within these institutions, as having opportunities for growth, for the integration of professional excellence and the deepening of their life? Why is it that they do not realize more fully Jesus Christ as the center of their life through their service and their coresponsible effort in the institution of higher learning? Is this part of a movement, for example, which is anti-intellectual? Is it part of a broader attitude which is known as anti-institutional? I do not know the answers to these questions. I ask you to explore them with me.

I do know some of the expectations of women religious around mission in the Catholic university or college. These expectations seem to range from a deep desire to see the tradition and the purposes of the founding Community preserved to a desire for an active consensus and commitment to these purposes. They range from a hope to experience faith community among faculty and students within the Catholic institution to the hope for an active and visible pastoral ministry within and beyond the institution itself. There is a strong desire for active, visible commitment to social justice as well as for professional excellence.

These expectations seem to me to speak of the need for a strong apostolic orientation within our colleges. They likewise challenge the ability of the college and university to meet the needs of the people and to prepare students to respond to these same needs, needs which are continually changing and shifting. I in no way see that these expectations minimize the importance of scholarly research. Rather they seem strongly to focus this very need. I do not hear or experience a desire for a dichotomy, for an either/or, but rather a both/and. We are aware that much of the tension which we know today around the nature and mission of the Catholic university and college results from change, change that has brought about a straining and refocusing of the stance of education itself. And just as the educational institution has strained and refocused, so too has the religious congregation experienced a changing and a shifting in its understanding of its mission.

Both the educational institution and the religious community have traditionally known a certain autonomy, a certain reality in themselves, and in the past these two have not been in opposition. Religious have found themselves deeply rooted in their religious values, in their gospel values of service within the institutions. Many have experienced our Catholic universities and colleges as a profound extension of the mission of their congregations. Yet today we hear the question, "Is my presence, is our presence in this particular college or university compatible with our mission?" Some sponsoring groups are asking whether they can continue sponsorship. Finance is certainly a primary factor, but I believe that this question is often asked in reference to the mission of the congregation and the ability of that institution to realize that mission.

This leads to another question: What is the emerging mission of women religious in today's world? Since the Second Vatican Council, when religious were urged to reflect on their life in light of the gospel, in light of their own history and traditions, and in light of the signs of the times, there has been a felt need for a shift from the traditional modes of service to newer forms of ministries, to ministry both within the institution and beyond it, to ministry which touches the needs of our people. There has been a strong emphasis on humanization of values, on peace, on justice. The impact of Vatican II in general, the continual exhortations of our Holy Father Paul VI, the thinking, the words of our bishops of the Synod of 1971 have had a profound effect on the response of women religious across our country. It is clear to us that education for justice is a primary concern of the Church and an integral part of her mission.

Is there any doubt that a new awareness has been raised in the Church, an awareness which points to a need for participation in promotion of peace and justice, an awareness of the need to liberate the oppressed? Are we not continually reminded that the promotion of peace and justice and the liberation of the oppressed are a constitutive element of the mission to which Jesus Christ has called his Church? I believe that this heightened awareness has been responsible for a noticeable shift in the understanding of the mission of women religious. Such a shift calls for a corporate response to social justice issues; it calls for a corporate commitment on the part of a congregation to deepen its understanding of justice. It demands serious reflection on the quality and form of our apostolic service, reflection on the nature of our commitment to Jesus Christ and to the mission of his Church. I believe that to the measure that Catholic universities and colleges promote this reflection and are actual agents of this kind of response to social needs, they will know the presence of women religious in the future.

The words of the bishops of the Synod of 1971 seem to provoke serious reflection in this regard:

> We have questioned ourselves about the mission of the people of God to further justice in the world. . . . Scrutinizing the "signs of the times" and seeking to detect the meaning of emerging history. . . we have listened to the Word of God that we might be converted to the fulfilling of the divine plan for the salvation of the world. . . . We have been able to perceive the serious injustices which are building. . . a network of domination, oppression, and abuses which stifle freedom and which keep the greater part of humanity from sharing in the building up and enjoyment of a more just. . . world. . . . At the same time we have noted the inmost stirring moving the world in its depths. There are facts constituting a contribution to the furthering of justice.

It seems to me that our colleges and our Catholic universities are called to be primary agents in helping the Church to realize this aspect of her mission. I believe that this call of the bishops speaks directly to the role, the nature and the mission of our universities and colleges, just as I strongly believe that the *Pastoral Constitution on the Church in the Modern World* (30) has a direct message for our educational institutions. It is that passage which is entitled, "More Than An Individualistic Ethic Is Required."

Profound and rapid changes make it particularly urgent that no one, ignoring the trend of events or drugged by laziness, content himself [or herself] with a merely individualistic morality. It grows increasingly true that the obligations of justice and love are fulfilled only if each person, contributing to the common good according to his [or her] own abilities and the needs of others, also promotes and assists the public and private institutions dedicated to bettering the conditions of human life. . . . Yet there are those who, while professing grand and rather noble sentiments, nevertheless in reality live always as if they cared nothing of the needs of society. . . . Let all consider it their sacred obligation to count social necessities among their primary duties and to pay heed to them. For the more unified the world becomes, the more plainly do the offices of all extend beyond particular groups and spread by degrees to the whole world. But this challenge cannot be met unless individual[s] . . . and their associations cultivate in themselves the moral and social virtues, and promote them in society.

After such reflection we might well ask what this says to the Catholic university, to the Catholic college, in the practical order. I believe that it says much to us about the mission of these institutions. It is obvious that many institutions are struggling to respond to the needs of their students, to develop a social rather than an individualistic ethic, to meet the life experience of their students. Sister Kathleen Feeley crystalized this so well, articulated it so clearly last night, as she described her own experience and the experience of the young women of her college, young women who find themselves in tension around the role of woman in the Church and in society today. This is a very serious question. It focuses a social issue, an issue which, as Sister Kathleen pointed out, touches the very life and future of religious communities. Beyond this I believe it touches in a very significant way the future of the Church and the ability of these young women to respond to the Church and its mission.

It seems to me that this is one of the issues which needs research, which demands the attention of the resources within our universities and our colleges. As our universities and colleges test their ability to respond to larger social questions, they continue to question their ability to cope with rapid social change, to communicate values. Their response will undoubtedly say much about the ability of the institutions of higher learning to be effective agents of evangelization. Inasmuch as students are ordinarily shaped by social patterns, it seems essential that in addition to scholarly research that our universities and colleges complement the efforts of the broader Church and the religious community, and the diverse efforts of our laity in raising social awareness, in providing for social processes, in increasing a sense of social responsibility, in developing a social ethic that will have meaning for the Church's mission in today's world and in the future.

I do not presume to say how this will be done, only that it *must* be done and that there must be a coresponsible effort among all of us who share the mission of Jesus Christ, the mission of his Church, to see that this *is* done. One of the ways which might help us would be an effort to call forth leadership within our universities and our colleges in an effort to bring individual institutions to academic honesty. Every institution cannot do everything. It seems, then, that there is a need for serious reflection on the part of each institution as to what it can do and what it cannot do, and as to what it can do differently. Bishop McManus quoted Fathery Orsy this morning in asking the question, "What is it that the college or the university can do truthfully as a Catholic institution?" I believe that that is a very important question.

There is no doubt that there is a real place for scholarly research. There is no doubt about the mission of the larger university, about the need for research centers, centers for theological and liturgical reflection. On the other hand, I believe there is also a real need for the small Catholic college. All institutions will not realize their mission in the same way. The basic purpose is the same. The ways of realizing that purpose will differ. I am reminded of a small diocesan college in which the needs of minority groups are met in a very unusual way, sixty-three percent of the student enrollment being minority groups. Contributed services of sisters from nine different communities make this effort possible. They are immediately responsible, coresponsible with one another for the realization of the religious mission of that educational institution.

I am sure that there are countless others that could be cited across our country. I am merely pointing out the need, not only to accept differences but to reverence them. I am also pointing out a need which Archbishop Borders cited last night, and that is the need to share what we have with one another. Perhaps at this point today all we have to share is vision, but I say, "Let us share it." I am reminded of the words of Habakkuk: "And Yahweh said, 'Write the vision down. Write it clearly upon the tablets so that it can be easily read.' " Another translation has it, "Write it in such a way that those who see it will run after it. That vision presses on to fulfillment. If it does not come, wait. It will come in time."

Let us share a willingness to wait, but also let us share a willingness to begin, to risk, to explore collaboration under the generic rubric of research, but beyond that, explore ways and means of redistributing our resources and reach out to minister to our people in a new way. Let us find ways through new structures, creative, interfacing, relational structures, structures which will enable us to talk to one another, to assist one another, to call one another, to be effective instruments in assisting the Church to realize her mission. Let us make an effort to create those structures which will give visibility to the relationship which exists among us, the relationship between the hierarchy and the educational institutions, the relationship between those serving in the institutions and those who are being served. Such structures will speak to the world of a shared mission in the Church of Jesus Christ and will help us continue to talk to one another and prayerfully reflect together in an effort to *be* the Church in the modern world.

Reflections On Cooperation
William J. Sullivan, S.J.

There are several comments and observations on the relation between the American Catholic Church and American Catholic higher education which I would like to share with you. These comments fall into two categories. First, observations that deal with conditions in the present situation which I consider to be enabling. There are some positive factors in the present situation of American colleges and universities which can contribute toward the kind of cooperation that we're talking about at this symposium. Secondly, observations on a set of conditions which tend to limit our efforts in this regard.

I turn first to the positive factors, the enabling conditions. One of these would be a growing sense in the academic community that every educational institution is, in some sense, a response to a societal need. Whether we're talking about a grade school, a Montessori kindergarten, or an institute for advanced studies, these institutions are in a very real sense of the word responses to the needs of society. I point to the obvious fact only for this reason: it seems to me to constitute the fundamental basis for the legitimacy of the Catholic community expressing to the academic community its needs. From the point of view of an academic administrator this kind of request, the making known of a group's needs, is in no sense of the word a taint upon the integrity of an academic institution. From my perspective, all educational institutions are responses to societal needs; what we have been talking about at this symposium is one aspect, one dimension of a societal need in the Roman Catholic community. Therefore, I find this kind of surfacing of needs and requests a legitimate and desirable enterprise.

Secondly, I would like to refer to something that Bishop McManus mentioned this morning. I agree with him that it is of little use to us to approach this question of the role of an academic institution by reflecting upon the "essence" of a college or a university or a research institute. I do not think that this category is very useful. I feel that colleges, universities, and research institutions should be thought of as social constructs, to use the language of the sociology of knowledge. To understand a college or university as a social construct implies that such an institution is malleable. We who are involved in these schools have a responsibility and an opportunity to build institutions that are attuned to and responsive to the kinds of societal needs and religious community needs that we're talking about at this symposium.

Thirdly, there is another enabling concept which has been very useful to me in my reflections on this issue. Dr. Quentin Quade, the Executive Vice President at Marquette University, has written several articles concerning the nature of a Catholic university. One of his basic observations was that there exists in any college or university setting, a whole series of what he calls "legitimate academic alternatives." Every educational institution, whether we're speaking about the University of California at Berkeley or Wheeling College in West Virginia, exercises options, makes choices in the area of its programs, its majors, its emphases. When a department or a college focuses its faculty resources, its research activity, its funding in a given direction, for example a particular form of economic theory or a particular kind of engineering, it is choosing according to its own goals and priorities a legitimate academic alternative. I think that this is an important concept for those of us who are academic administrators because it emphasizes the legitimacy of an educational institution in the Catholic tradition, focusing on the kind of concerns which have occupied us here, namely, the Catholic identity, the Catholic tradition, or the specific needs of the Catholic community. To do this is not in any sense of the word to violate the nature or the traditions of the university or college.

Let me very briefly point to a fourth present condition which I think is a positive one. This condition results from the phenomenal growth in the American educational community of adult and continuing education, extension education and non-traditional education. Very few American institutions of higher education today have not gone into this type of education in a massive way. Again there seems to me to be a very interesting fit between the continuing education orientation which many educational institutions have assumed and the kinds of opportunities, constituencies, and needs that we're talking about here. If we had discussed this topic ten years ago, such cooperation would have been regarded as much more peripheral to the operation of the educational institution than it is today. At that time institutions tended to be defined much more narrowly in terms of curriculum and the age categories that they were serving. These perceptions have given way to a more extended sense of the institution and of its educational operations. And this I find to be very reinforcing for the types of relations we are speaking of here.

Those four elements I consider to be enabling, i.e., positive, contributory factors, in our present situation. Let me now discuss several other factors or conditions which can be seen as limiting, or potentially limiting, to this whole cooperative enterprise.

The first limiting factor, which Bishop McManus referred to earlier in his quotation from Father Orsy, is the matter of personnel. If you or I or any other academic administrator here had the opportunity to go out today and recruit the personnel that we wanted, if we could fly around the country and select 50 or 150 or 250 faculty members with this cooperative task in mind, we could obviously put together a faculty that would have tremendous responsiveness and potential in this dimension. Our limitation comes from the fact that we have faculty in place and that the mobility and flexibility of those faculties is often very limited. Why? As a spokesman from the academic side, I would have to say honestly that a large part of the lack of responsiveness to these issues which we might find today in our faculties is due to the fact that over a fairly extended period of time the expansion of our schools and recruitment of faculties was done under different conditions and with different perspectives in mind. We frequently hired people without any concern for the ideological, philosophical, and religious values and attitudes which those people brought to our faculties. One example which comes to mind from my own personal experience is the case of one outstanding faculty member at St. Louis University.

This individual is a non-Catholic. He recounts that when he was interviewed at St. Louis University, he was assured that it did not make the slightest difference that it was a Catholic and Jesuit institution. After making an enormous contribution to the student life at St. Louis University as a faculty member for almost ten years, he says very clearly "it does make a difference. It made a difference to me; I'm a different kind of person today because this is a Catholic institution."

In addition to the presence in our institutions of faculty members who are not interested in this aspect of the educational mission, there is the matter of limitation on further faculty selection. As all of you know, all educational institutions and all administrators are under directives relating to affirmative action in hiring. What is not widely realized is that according to these regulations and interpretations an educational institution is forbidden to make hiring distinctions on the basis of religion. One cannot hire an individual for a faculty or administrative position because he or she is, or is not, a Catholic. This is a complex topic and needs much development and clarification, but it can be seen as a limitation on the hiring of personnel who would be interested in or sympathetic to this mission of cooperation with and service to the needs of the Catholic community.

A second limiting condition which I think has to be mentioned, if we are going to be realistic, is the question of funding. With all the interest and all the goodwill that we have in an opportunity for cooperation, when we approach the question of the contribution of Catholic colleges and universities to this sort of endeavor, we traditionally approach this question from the point of view of overload. We ask what can this institution and its faculty and administrators do in addition to their regular work. I think that in doing so we are really building in a condition that is going to destroy the whole operation over a period of time. I do not think that it is realistic nor equitable to approach this question from the point of overload.

Therefore, the question of funding is a very important and very serious one, particularly with respect to what sources of new funding are available to the hierarchy, to the national Catholic organizations, and to the individual diocese which would enable the Catholic college or university to engage in this sort of work. Dr. Noonan yesterday offered to the symposium some figures concerning financial support for a research institute. I have been trying to do a bit of mental calculation myself; it seems to me that if the Catholic colleges and universities in this country had available as support for these kinds of operations funding equivalent to only one-tenth of one percent of their normal operating budgets, they could do a number of positive and significant things. Those of you who are administrators might calculate that figure in relation to your own school's budget. My very rough calculations would be that this proposal would amount to somewhere in the area of two million dollars nationally. This is only a part of the annual revenues that are available to the several Catholic foundations that are represented at this symposium. Two million dollars is not a lot of money, and I believe that if such an amount were at our disposal, our institutions would be enabled to carry on the various cooperative activities which otherwise become an overload strain.

We now approach a third and final point. There are many limitations

in the potential for cooperation due to the official, we might say even episcopal, attitudes toward Catholic colleges and universities. After reflecting on this matter for some time and determining what I wanted to say, I came to this morning's session and listened to Bishop McManus express, from his point of view, a number of the things that I wanted to say from my point of view as an academic administrator. Specifically, one of my critical concerns is the very important question of the attitude of the local episcopacy toward the Catholic college and university. In his own marvelous way of putting it, Bishop McManus refers to "calling upon the episcopacy to authenticate and support, rather than to criticize and tear down, the efforts of those who are working within the diocese, whether it's in a very small college or in a larger university."
The tremendous importance that the local bishop and the local pastors can have in the area of recruiting Catholic students for these institutions is a very clear example of such support. The attitude of the bishops and pastors can be a major factor in the presence or absence of Catholic students within those schools.

Thirdly, there is the related question of deliberate and systematic efforts to use the Catholic institutions and their resources for diocesan projects and needs. In a day in which one of the major problems of most Catholic schools is underutilization of resources, it is a very important kind of gesture for the diocese to engage this school directly in its own activities and projects.

Finally, I would like to mention another matter that affects cooperation. This matter is the great support, the very critical support, that can be offered by the American Catholic hierarchy on a number of issues touching the relationship between the Catholic universities and colleges and the Church. I would refer briefly to two examples. It appears, in my very limited and fallible judgment, that an effort is being made by the Roman congregation to move away from the decisions that were made several years ago about the independence and legitimate relative autonomy of Catholic universities and colleges. This attempt is seen through a series of requirements and demands which have been made public in the course of this past summer and are now under discussion. It is my judgment that an attempt to reverse these prior decisions represents a retrograde position with regard to the Catholic higher education system of this country. It represents one more aspect of the regressive phase through which the Roman Catholic Church is now passing. As an administrator at a university under that system, I am anxiously waiting to see whether the American Catholic hierarchy will or will not as a body publicly and vigorously defend that college and university system which is absolutely unique in the world and in the Roman Catholic Church. If such support does not materialize, this will undoubtedly limit the effectiveness of the Catholic institutions of higher learning in general and the cooperation between school and Church which we are all seeking to foster.

Will we or will we not be cut to pieces by the attempts of the Roman congregation to go into a retrograde position? Will or will not the bishops who know us and know our positions in this country, publicly and vigorously deal with Rome on that issue? That is something which I, as just one individual, await with great anticipation.

In speaking of episcopal attitude, one other issue needs to be discussed. It concerns the unjust, immoral, and illegitimate regulations of the Roman congregations regarding the hiring of ex-priests by the theology departments of Catholic schools. I believe it is a violation of the human rights of those persons and a violation of the relative autonomy of those institutions for a Roman congregation to decree that none of these individuals can be hired by a Catholic institution. The hiring or non-hiring in such cases should be the result of the responsible decision of the legitimate authority within the institution. Here again I have heard nothing stated publicly or corporately from the American Catholic bishops that would lead me to think that they want to deal with this issue as it appears within the American context.

These, therefore, are some of what I consider to be the limiting factors in our response to the needs of the American Catholic community; I mention them only out of the desire to be realistic. We do have serious limitations of personnel, of funding, and of attitude.

Let me end by expressing a personal note of appreciation to all the bishops who came to this symposium and took part in the discussion, giving their time and attention to a very important topic. Finally, let me say very honestly, as one person who has been working and continues to work in the apostolate of Catholic higher education, I do not think that we Catholic college and university administrators can promise that we will be able to continue this work successfully and effectively under the extraordinary financial pressures we are experiencing, under the increasing direct competition from the state education sector, and under the pressures of state and federal regulatory agencies if we do not have more comprehension and support from the hierarchical voices within the Catholic community itself.

The Catholic Academic Community in the Service of the Church

Evelyn Eaton Whitehead

As I assess our plenary sessions and small group discussions during this symposium, it seems we have spent some considerable time together in consideration of the Catholic academic community in its relation to the Church—one of the institutional environments within which it functions and to which it is responsible. I would like to focus my comments on another environment within which the Catholic academic community functions—the institutional system of higher education within the United States.

Most generally, the term "higher education" designates those social institutions concerned with the public quest for knowledge—its acquisition, transmission, certification and application. The term, however, is more likely to be used in a somewhat narrower sense to refer particularly to the model that serves as the core of the American post-secondary education system—the university with a graduate school and a research faculty. The point has been well made, by Talcott Parsons and Gerald Platt in their recent analysis of *The American University* as well as by others, that this graduate school and research model serves as a norm of higher education. Thus, appropriately or not, the goals, objectives and criteria of the graduate school function as significant influences upon the other forms of postsecondary education in our society—such as the liberal arts college, the denominational or religiously-affiliated institution, the professional or vocational school. It is this influence upon the Catholic college and university of the norms of the broader American university system that I wish to draw to our attention.

In America today the university system serves a number of important societal functions. I shall mention here several that are of significance.

A central task of the institutions of higher education in any society is to safeguard the canons and methods of rational thinking accepted by the society. In the contemporary American university this responsibility finds expression in a commitment to the standards of cognitive rationality, the requirement for the objective grounding of propositions, and the quest for conceptual clarity and logical validity. A second objective of the university is the use of these methods of rational thinking to acquire new knowledge (through research and other forms of scholarship) and to transmit the society's intellectual heritage (through teaching and writing).

In addition to these more obvious and often articulated goals, the university has other socially important functions as well. In its role as educator of an important minority of 18–22 year olds, the university is a major socializing agent for the elite of the next generation. The university does not only "inform the mind." Acknowledged or not, the influence of the university experience upon the values and even the character of its students is often significant and, even where the role of transmitter of values and molder of character is publically disavowed, is not unintended. The experience of higher education reinforces for students society's expectations about the good life, citizenship, personal responsibility, achievement and success—and provides criteria by which these are evaluated.

In addition, the university is often seen, especially by the business and civic community, as responsible for providing to society sufficient numbers of persons with the range of intellectual and technical skills required to serve the needs of the society. And finally, but surely not unimportantly, the American university system is an employer of some modest importance in the economy.

We might at this point turn our consideration immediately to detailing the degree to which Catholic colleges and universities do—or should—serve comparable functions in the life of the Catholic Christian Church. Whether they do, or should, establish and maintain intellectual standards for Catholic or Christian thinking; whether they do, or should, socialize the next generation into an explicitly Catholic culture; whether they do, or should, provide to the Church sufficient numbers of persons motivated and skilled to carry on the ministeries, roles, and services of the Church. But instead I want to stay with my original focus—consideration of ways in which the dominant model of university education in the United States serves as an environment influencing Catholic colleges and universities in regard to their self-understanding and their activities.

There are at least two differing evaluations of the relationship that might exist between this dominant model of higher education in the United States, as I have sketched it above, and the religious enterprise or the pastoral mission of the Church. On the one hand, religion can be understood as the antagonist of higher education. In such an evaluation, the objectives of higher education are judged to be antithetical to religious faith and humane values. The contemporary university is seen to be characterized by narrow definitions of knowledge and truth, an exclusive commitment to cognitive rationality, and the dominance of the scientific method. It is seen to function through a dehumanizing system of bureaucratic structures, insensitive to the experience and initiative of students, faculty and staff alike.

Such a negative appraisal of the contemporary American university is found not only among its religious critics outside the system. A scholar of the stature of Robert Bellah, whose credential and contribution within the system are unassailable, voices a similar judgment.

In the face of a system of higher education that would merit such a description, the Church might be called to a prophetic stance—its function to challenge the goals and actions of the university, to safeguard and buttress the important religious and human values that are under attack in the alien university environment. An independent system of Catholic colleges and universities might be the vehicle of such a stance.

To be sure, an alternate evaluation of the relationship between religion and the American system of higher education is possible. A reverence for learning and an accompanying concern for the forms and institutions of higher education are part of a long religious tradition for Catholic Christianity. The university and the Church can be seen as sharing some central value commitments—the conviction that knowledge can be a path to transcendence, that the pursuit of truths is a way to Truth, that education is a means to freedom and human betterment.

Where this judgment of shared values can be made, the pastoral mission of the Church can include a commitment to facilitate, assist, and influence the university's pursuit of its own educational goals. In such a stance, the central tasks of the university—formulating and communicating knowledge, educating and socializing students, preparing professional practitioners in the competencies required to carry on society's business—can be viewed as activities appropriate to the pastoral function of the Church and deserving of collaboration and support.

These two evaluations might be seen as poles of a continuum along which most of us would place ourselves, in regard to our own appraisal of the relationship between the institutional functions proper to the university and the pastoral mission of the Church.

In our conference discussions here we have heard the Catholic college and university challenged—at the level of both their honesty and creativity—to reassert their Catholic identity and to serve more vigorously in the pastoral mission of the Church. As we in the academic community marshal our resources of wit and ingenuity to respond to this challenge, we are also aware of similar pressures from the other side—pressures to accept and to conform to the standards of academic endeavor and excellence as defined by the broader American experience of university education. Represented in the requirements of accrediting agencies, the expectations of many of the best members of our faculties, and the demands of foundations and other sources of financial support, these pressures from the secular establishment are likely to increase rather than to diminish over the immediate future. In some important sense our effective service within and beyond the Catholic community will depend on our ability to mediate the legitimate demands of this educational establishment as well as those of the Church.

I would like to move now to a consideration of the terms in which American colleges and universities speak of their own goals and functions, in order to indicate, with examples drawn largely from the discussions of this symposium, areas of potential overlap between these goals and the pastoral mission of the Church.

College and university statements generally include explicit reference to three institutional goals. These are research and scholarship, instruction, and service. Research is concerned with the enlargement of knowledge through the discovery of what was previously unknown and the development of insights, models, and theories for better understanding of what is known. Scholarship, a goal which in some statements of purpose is left implicit under the more general rubric of ''research,'' is directed toward the assimilation and preservation (as distinguished from the enlargement) of accumulated knowledge, and experience. Instruction is concerned with the transmission of knowledge, experience, and understanding.

References to the goal of public service may be found in the literature of virtually every institution of higher education. This service goal is subject to various interpretations and seldom merits the resources of personnel or planning that other institutional functions do. In the United States, however, the initial foundation of many colleges and universities has been directly related to the public service that it was understood these institutions would perform. For example, Harvard—our country's first college—was established to provide a learned clergy for the early communities of New England. The land grant colleges, many now universities, which form an important part of the higher education system in many states, carried an initial mandate of service to the needs of the local areas in which they were established. And Catholic colleges and universities have almost universally spoken of themselves as participants in the work and witness of Christ and as at the service of his Church.

These three goals proper to the enterprise of higher education may serve as a framework for our consideration of the areas of legitimate overlap between the functions of the Catholic college and university and the pastoral mission of the Church. It is not my intent to undertake an original or complete listing of projects or programs which have been or might be undertaken by Catholic institutions to expand their collaboration in the pastoral mission. Such is the task of this symposium's smaller working groups. I will simply point to several of the suggestions that have already arisen in our discussions here.

Touching the goal of instruction we have received three proposals in regard to undergraduate education. Sister Barbara Thomas has urged a curriculum that would educate to social ethics and public responsibility. Father Hesburgh has alerted us to the task of overcoming the religious and theological illiteracy of many of our students. Dr. Noonan has challenged at least one institution among us to establish an undergraduate college of highest excellence, rigor, and breadth which might serve as a seed ground for the development of Catholic scholars for the Church of the twenty-first century.

Catholic graduate and professional schools have been reinforced in their efforts to provide a next generation of scholars, teachers, lawyers, ministers, medical professionals, and business men and women with both the religious sensitivity and the professional skills necessary for effective service to the needs of the human community beyond and within the Church.

The consideration of possible collaboration of the Catholic academic community in the pastoral mission of the Church through research has involved us in discussion of even greater range. We have received Dr. Noonan's description of an elite research institution dedicated to the careful, systematic, patient study of one or more basic issues of important theological and human consequence. From several quarters there has also been the call for many Catholic institutions and individual scholars to undertake and foster studies that will contribute to the understanding and, hopefully, the resolution of human and ecclesial problems with which the pastors and bishops of the Church deal daily.

82

Regarding the services which the Catholic college and university might offer to others in the Church, we have heard suggestions of how their resources—knowledge, personnel, facilities—might be made increasingly available. Catholic scholars in a number of fields might serve, as individuals or as a more formal commision, as resource persons to bishops or diocesan pastoral planning councils. Catholic intellectuals might take on the interpretive task of translating the facts, findings and methods of their academic disciplines to make them more realistically available to those involved in areas of practical action. Catholic colleges and universities might initiate or provide resources for programs of adult religious education and continuing professional education for those involved in the ministries of the local Church.

This somewhat schematized summary of initiatives already on the floor of this conference should reinforce our hope for the developing collaboration between Catholic institutions of higher education and bishops in the pastoral mission of the Church. Tonight's final reports from the conference work groups will give further substance to this hope.

Many of us have remarked on the enthusiasm for collaboration between bishops and members of the Catholic academic community that we have experienced here. There is a feeling that both parties may well benefit—to the ultimate service of the Church and the human community. There are, no doubt, cautions that each of us continues to carry along with our enthusiasm. In closing I want to articulate a caution of my own. It is a reminder first, of course, to myself. It may be useful as well in our common conversation.

Let us be appropriately modest about the contribution that the Catholic academic community can make to the pastoral mission of the Church. There is good theological tradition urging this modesty. We know—by faith and, most of us, by experience as well—that without God's enabling grace even our best efforts are fruitless. But I mention my caution here based less on theological grounds than on the witness of recent experience. I will cite two cases.

In the establishment of the nation of Israel over the past 25 years, systematic effort was made to involve the substantial intellectual resources of the American and European Jewish community in planning and problem solving. The response of the Jewish intellectual community has been generous. And yet a conviction that has grown among many Jewish scholars involved in this social experiment is that the effectiveness of their own best efforts has been small.

In the recent political history of our own country—exemplified in the New Frontier of the Kennedy era and the Great Society of the Johnson administration—we have seen the "best and the brightest" of an important segment of American intellectual life marshalled in the service of the nation. Events of the last five years have brought us to a period of widespread skepticism concerning the value of the contribution we can expect from the academic world.

I do not wish to underplay the important contributions that have been made by scholars and intellectuals to moral purpose and democratic activity in our time. I mean rather to recall for us all that the understanding and appreciation of the human condition seem to transcend the tools and talents of any one so specialized group. The practical complexity of social life and human purpose is not necessarily deciphered more easily or accurately by the academic than by the poet, politician, or parishioner.

In the opening address of this symposium Archbishop Bernadin reminded us that the Word of God has been given to the whole Church, not simply to those who serve through the magisterium. Let me say here, then, that the wisdom and compassion that will be required of us as we attempt a faithful witness to Christ in our own time is also given, through the Spirit, to the whole Church.

But with this one caution enunciated, let me return to share in the enthusiasm that has been engendered among us through the discussions and fellowship of these two days. Our closer collaboration—as bishops and intellectuals—is to be welcomed. And we have begun.

Solemn Vespers:
Homily
Most Rev. Edmund C. Szoka

The passage from the Acts of the Apostles—Acts 9:20–30—which we have just heard read, relates the events which immediately followed St. Paul's conversion to Christ. He had experienced an extraordinary, overwhelming event which he would never forget. In the midst of a flashing light he had seen the Lord and had conversed with him. For three days afterwards he had been blinded and had to be led by the hand until the Lord sent Ananias to restore his sight. When the scales fell from his eyes, he rose and was baptized. From that day on, Paul became the greatest of all evangelists, more pastorally present to the society of his day than we can even begin to imagine. His success as missionary, scholar, writer, theologian, mystic, and administrator has been unparalleled in Christian history. As he himself tells us, the key to that astounding success was his deep, abiding faith which grew to such perfect union with Christ that he could say with complete honesty: "Life to me, of course, is Christ" (Phil. 1:21).

Saul, the Jewish boy in the Hellinist city of Tarsus, was certainly exposed to the Greek language and culture of his environment. As he himself said, he came from "no mean city." As a young man, he went to the temple college in Jerusalem to study under the venerated Gamaliel and eventually became a rabbi of the Pharisaic school.

At the time of his conversion, he had been a dedicated, zealous persecutor of the Christian sect. However, from the moment of his dramatic meeting with Christ, his conversion was total, complete, and permanent. Shortly after that conversion, he began to proclaim in the synagogues of Damascus that Jesus was the Son of God. His presentations were not little pious sermonettes because, as our passage reads, he "grew steadily more powerful and reduced the Jewish community of Damascus to silence with his proofs that Jesus was the Messiah."

However, he was not universally accepted. After three years, certain Jews conspired to kill him and Paul was forced to flee. He made his way to Jerusalem, his first trip to that city since his conversion. He tried to join the disciples there but they wouldn't accept him because they were all afraid of him. Barnabas came to his rescue and introduced him to the apostles. They accepted him because they were convinced of the sincerity of his faith. He had seen the Lord and had publicly given witness to his faith. That was enough for them. They required nothing more.

St. Paul eventually moved out into the Gentile world and became the missionary to the Gentiles. His three great missionary journeys were blessed with outstanding success. But they were not free of suffering. He was rejected by his own; he was scourged, beaten, driven out of town. He was shipwrecked. He had problems with one of his co-evangelists. He even had some problems with Peter over dietary laws.

Yet Paul never wavered. He never turned back. Instead he kept growing in his union with Christ. He became so identified with Christ that he could say without pride or conceit, "Be imitators of me as I am of Christ" (1 Cor. 11:1).

He kept traveling, he kept preaching, he kept debating, he kept organizing local churches. But perhaps most importantly for us, he wrote his inspired letters. In spite of the many centuries of their existence, his writings are still the object of profound and inexhaustible study by the theologians and scripture scholars of the world. His letters, too, have never ceased during all this time to move and edify Christians of all cultures and nationalities. And in a special way, they have occupied the attention of the greatest mystics in their search for perfect union with Christ.

In the context of the symposium for which we have come to Notre Dame, St. Paul has pointed the way for our efforts. He was able to "transplant Christianity, without destroying any of its roots, from the ancient earth of Israel to fertile, Gentile soil."

Paul's life, however, reveals an even more profound role. It is clear that all great movements "are initiated and sustained by ideas." As one writer put it,

> Paul's is not merely intellectual genius; his is a vision of
> God's saving activity joined and compenetrated into man's
> entire human existence. For Paul, a man of many worlds,

Christianity is no isolation. Jew, Greek, Roman, workman, intellectual, evangelist—through unbelievable hardships and great joys—all brought Paul, the many faceted personality, to drink deeply of the death-and-resurrection mystery of Christ.

Only men and women of deep faith whose life, work, study, and experience have brought them to drink deeply of the death-and-resurrection mystery of Christ can produce the ideas to nourish the movement of evangelization in the American context. There is no other way.

The task we are about is no mere human task. To treat it as such would mean commitment to failure. St. Paul tells us why in his first letter to the Corinthians:

Make no mistake about it: if any one of you thinks of himself as wise, in the ordinary sense of the word, then he must learn to be a fool before he really can be wise. Why? Because the wisdom of this world is foolishness to God (1 Cor. 3:18–19).

IV. PLENARY SESSION
January 13

Reports of Group Discussions

DISCUSSION GROUP ONE:
THE LOCAL CHURCH VIS-À-VIS
NEIGHBORHOOD AND SOCIETY

David O'Brien, Reporter

We began with the realization of the importance and centrality of the parish in the life of the Church, referring specifically to the remarks of Bishop Ottenweller at the recent bishops meeting. Both among religious educational professionals and people active in social action, there is a growing realization of the importance of the primary Christian community. The work of all such groups depends as does the whole Church on the strength and vitality of the local Church.

Drawing on a vast amount of experience among our participants, we discussed three different ways of building community. One, an effort to develop fellowship in the Church with an emphasis upon greater spontaneity. Two, developing community by emphasis upon the common faith experience of the participants. Three, developing community by bringing people together around common action and a shared mission of the Church. A distinction arose between the potential service to the Church of the university, with its research capability; and that of a small college with fewer resources but perhaps a greater capability of integrating itself creatively with its neighborhood and region and perhaps less built-in resistance to responding to the local community or to the local Church.

Several examples of cooperation action emerged. One was efforts in campus ministry work to utilize campus parishes as centers for the liturgical innovation, testing grounds for new pastoral strategies. Such communities also offer the students an opportunity to participate and share first hand with families in building faith communities, organizing liturgy, and conducting the religious education of children. A second example was offered by several descriptions of efforts to share the local colleges with their neighborhoods in facing and gaining control over the processes of social change at work around them. By carefully placing some of their resources at the disposal of the community, some small colleges have won community support and elaborated their services in the area. A third model was that of schools serving as training centers for religious education, working closely with pastors, coordinators, and religious education committees. This model has the added benefit in some cases of providing an opportunity for service for the priest who has been away for academic training and is frustrated in normal parish work. Another model was provided by those colleges and universities which seek to offer training to seminarians in specific skills which were often not available to them in their seminary work, such skills as education, music, accounting, group dynamics, and group process.

Another point emphasized was the ability of Catholic colleges and universities to participate in a continuing education of priests and people, particularly in adult education work in which Church and college could cooperate. This provides the scholar. with a way of having his knowledge reach the grassroots and can give flesh to the colleges' often-acknowledged sense of responsibility to the local Church. Another point emphasized by some of the academics was the ability of such Church institutions as hospitals, parishes, social service agencies, to provide an experiencial component in the training and education of undergraduate students.

Several participants emphasized the existence of a large body of social teaching which many of our bishops have thought through and are incorporating in their statements at the national level, but that priests and people have not yet confronted. In the effort to bring to the attention of lay people and clergy the existence and significance and implications of this emerging social theology, lies an area for potential cooperation between the academic and pastoral sides of the Church. Especially needed are new educational strategies which will integrate social and pastoral life of the church and help people articulate their experience and integrate into their experience the insights of contemporary social theology.

Perhaps most important, both the bishops and the leaders of the academic community in our group recognize that we are in midst of rapid change both in the self-understanding of the Church in its own faith and in terms of the concrete social situation of our people, as they leave behind the old neighborhoods and the old parish. Working together, those who study the Church and those who lead it must help shape a new vision and define a new set of possibilities, must help form, in Archbishop Borders' words, "new combinations of faith community and sociological community." Concrete Proposals:

1. The need for diocesan-wide consultations, similar to the present meeting. Scholars, academic officials, and bishops need to come to a better understanding of each other's needs and to make known the resources that they can offer to one another. This consultation should be carried out on all sides with a great deal of sensitivity to the needs, concerns and feelings of those on the other side.

2. The appointment of a liaison person in the diocese, whose task it would be to make contact with and establish friendships with people in universities, would be most beneficial in the long run, or to both sides.

3. The production of an index of local campus resources would be of benefit to the Church.

4. Areas of immediate collaboration, include continuing education of clergy and adults, neighborhood development, and the study of family structures, family education, and family services, to be carried out in association with family service agencies in the local Church.

5. It would be useful for those interested in promoting this collaboration to choose one diocese as a pilot model. This diocese should have an interested episcopal leadership and the openness on the part of some colleges and university administrations to such cooperation. It should be one in which processes of pastoral consultation are already well developed, and in which there are some structures presently existing for pastoral planning and pastoral renewal. Within such a diocese we would like to see programs developed in five different types of parishes: inner city, ethnic-working class, suburban, and alternative parishes together with rural parish. These models, packaged and presented attractively, might be of benefit to people in other parts of the country. Some people in our group felt that Newark offered such a model, for the bishop is new, there is a desire to break new ground, and Seton Hall University has always been most cooperative with its diocese.

DISCUSSION GROUP TWO:
CATHOLIC IDENTITIES

Michael Novak, Reporter

Our first act was to change the title to the plural: Catholic *Identities*. If we stop to think for a moment of all our own families and relatives, then of the spread of American Catholics—everybody from a Mario Savio to a Carroll O'Connor, from Bill Buckley to a Jimmy Breslin, Frank Sinatra and Abigail McCarthy, Ella Grasso and Mike Mansfield, George Blanda and George Meany—you have some sense of what a complicated body of people we are trying to represent.

The question of Catholic identities in relation to the problems of the bishops and the universities reveals certain constraints:

1. Economic Constraints. What special role, what special goods, do Catholic schools have to offer, so that people will be willing to pay the extra money that it costs? A crucial question because of tax rulings.

2. Constraints Regarding Personnel. If for the past twenty years a number of Catholic colleges—most—have striven for a greater excellence according to standards of our society, have they drifted farther from their specific Catholic identity? So, at many Catholic colleges, concern about *Catholic* things is now part of a subculture, rather than part of the identity of the colleges as a whole. It may be built in through tenure, through the kind of faculty recruited.

3. Conceptual Constraints. (a) One model, more concerned with orthodoxy and a kind of doctrinal emphasis, and turning down state funds in order to maintain identity. (b) Another college, carefully studying the law, making legal adjustments, on the grounds it is preferable to stay in existence and remain competitive, until we have a different Supreme Court or different political climate. (c) Between those two, a third, trying not to make merely legal adjustments and yet trying to fight the courts. Can it be, in this country, that you cannot be Catholic and also qualify for normal public support? Can there be that kind of inhospitality?

4. Cultural Constraints. We work in a mainstream which is not in its assumptions, or in its elites, or in its symbols, Catholic. We have also a problem of cultural constraints with our own people. It is not clear what relationships either the bishops or the Catholic universities have with the actual concrete Catholic cultures of this country.

5. Constraints of Competition. Catholic schools in competition with each other; with state schools; with private schools, both nonreligious and religious though not Catholic.

In addition, there are questions we can hardly have begun to discuss, involving the problems more internal to ourselves. First, personally, what is it that makes persons—all 50 million of us—Catholic; what does it add to one's identity? Second, communally, what is added by a Catholic community; what are its strengths and weaknesses, as in a Catholic college? Third, is there such a thing as a Catholic culture or cultures? Because we have theological interests, we tend to put down sociological Catholicism in favor of what we call "authentic Catholicism." But what if that sociological Catholicism is itself very strong, very potent, a carrier of theological meaning? What if there is a lot more integrity in that culture, all implicit as it is, than we recognize?

Then there are two issues that Archbishop Bernardin brought up: One, the *theological-moral* identity. In our new technology and new culture, what anthropology do we have, what wisdom, that is specifically Catholic, that shows some theological and moral power that differentiates us? And how can we articulate it? The other, the *political-social* dimension. Supposing we had a clear self-understanding and we wanted to strengthen our institutions, our cultural networks, and our theological vision, both for all those Catholics who are not in Catholic colleges and for those who are: do we have the social and political potency to achieve politically and socially what we think we want and what we think we deserve?

Issues to be Explored

Kathleen Feeley, S.N.D., Reporter

A. What elements are necessary for colleges to be a resource for a diocesan evangelization program?
1. Constitutional question vs. Catholic identity and government funding. More development of "Free Exercise" clause.
2. Mechanism necessary for such cooperation.
3. Inventory of capabilities. A major role might be to study Catholic people in the American context: immigrant history, immigrant literary activity; oral history projects; census questions; history of the diocese.
4. Funding. Such work cannot be an "overload" for faculties. It

could be done under "joint appointment" of college and diocese. Possibility of "contributed services" to be allotted to special fund for such purposes.

5. Pastoral Policy. Research should have an impact on pastoral policy. Organizational measures should insure that research be truly utilized.

6. Curriculum. Should we be studying Catholic culture as part of a liberal arts curriculum? A Catholic studies program?

B. How can Catholic women assume a stronger leadership role in the Woman's Movement?

1. Women should exercise leadership in deepening this movement to one of true human freedom for service wherever one's talents indicate.

2. Women should sensitize men to a deeper understanding of the Woman's Movement. Then men in turn will sensitize other men.

3. The media is shaping our view of the Woman's Movement. We should try to influence the media.

DISCUSSION GROUP THREE: PRAYER AND SPIRITUAL FORMATION

Clyde F. Crews, Reporter

Within the context of spirituality, the question we asked was, how can the Catholic institution of higher learning be involved in the evangelization work of the Church. We extended the notion of the college and the university to include the seminaries and possibly the novitiate institutes as well. These are obviously significant groups which we have not been mentioning. So we use the phrase, the Catholic *schola*, meaning those four types of institutions, as we go through this discussion. Also, we tried to draw together some meaning for the phrase evangelization. To attempt a brief definition, it has to do with sharing with others, especially those with no previous contact, the power and the presence and the energy and the value and the work that Christ came to spread to the earth; sharing those qualities among others, especially those who had not come in contact with them previously.

With those two points, as kind of a background, we looked first at the mission of the Catholic schola. This conference has shown significant agreement on the mission of the Catholic schola. It is a place where the thinking work of the Church is done, especially in theology and philosophy; it is a place where people are prepared for the service work—that is, both within the Church and to the world; it is a place for the alerting of conscience and for the widening of awareness of a community and the world. It is a place where people are brought forth, both faculty and students, who can make a degree of difference in the world. They make those values and concerns that are identified in Christian tradition, especially in Catholic tradition, evident in the midst of their community. If you will, they are a kind of counter-culture, who look carefully at society, at the Church, and at themselves. And finally the people who are produced by such an institution revere the special tradition which is theirs and approach such a tradition loyally and critically and creatively.

Making such assumptions about the general mission of the Catholic schola, our second major point was a special consideration of the spiritual work of the Catholic schola. Before the Catholic schola can evangelize anyone, before it can help a diocese or a bishop or a world, it needs to be constantly evangelizing its own self, especially with regard to its own spirituality. In saying this we kept in mind the very special strengths that we tried to identify. We tried to pinpoint some of the special strength we saw in Catholic spirituality and theology. These included a special understanding of the relationship of faith and reason; a very acute concern for justice as a constitutive part of the Gospel; the mystical tradition of the Church; and the history of the Church, because any group that is trying to have its identity and trying to make a difference in the community becomes very conscious of its history. When we mention the history of Catholicism in particular, it points us to the fact that the Catholic tradition is integrative; that is, it joins together prayer and spirituality, worship and intellect, art and emotion, compassion and social justice; and it has those fascinating people called the saints around, who give flesh and blood form to the grand ideas of which we have been speaking.

One thing we struggled with was the many meanings of prayer, trying to come up with a good definition. We did not want to be exclusive. We were quite aware that prayer can mean liturgy; it can mean work in the world; we used the concept of Schillebeeckx of sacred liturgy and secular liturgy, both must be involved. We do need a place where people can experience good liturgy and learn the meaning of the integrating force of prayer, especially private prayer, as a special need in our time. We developed certain guide thoughts for a spirituality center, a program in private prayer that could quite properly be put under the auspices of many of the Catholic schola. There is a need in the Church for spiritual discipline to develop the attitudes of heart and mind so that people can fruitfully participate in the Eucharist. If in fact it is the center of Catholic life, then it does not stand on its own. People must come to the Eucharist prepared for it. So a need for a spiritual discipline to develop attitudes of heart and mind to participate fruitfully in the Eucharist.

Secondly we saw a need specific to our day; how to center and be still with the Lord, to make decisions regarding priorities and the use of time; a need to discover the integrative power of prayer in building up the community life of faculty and students. We wanted to underline faculty because we were aware that we were going to have to speak to our own people first. When we talk about self-evangelizing, maybe the faculty need it even more than the students. Only then, having tidied up our own house in this continuing process, do we think about sharing with the community at large. We recognized certain suspicions would inevitably arise if we develop such a program in private prayer. One would be the question that should and would immediately be raised, ''Is this just a return to individualism? Is this a denial of the social action component of the Church?'' The second problem that might be brought up is, ''Does it represent a loss of academic rigor?'' In other words, is everyone going to go into his closet now and pray privately and let the academic world go by? Obviously the kinds of things we are proposing would have to meet those objections.

What do we do about areas that do not have Catholic schola— universities, colleges, seminaries, novitiates? We talked about setting up institutes, possibly summer institutes that might be staffed by other Catholic colleges, or by resource people from other Catholic colleges. The significant comment was made that these colleges doing the providing would probably get the most benefit from it in the pastoral situation, getting off the campus, and working very closely in a diocese in this way. We also proposed an institute in spirituality that could be formed on several campuses; the need for liturgical centers, which are already set up in some places. We also recognized the need of faculty members who have a special sense of the task of the Catholic schola. In recruiting faculty members we must learn how to find out whether their sensitivities are the same as the institution's; especially with regard to spirituality and social task.

In summary then, we recognized an increasing sense of the importance of prayer and communities of prayer in people's lives today. That is an unavoidable fact. There is a growing sense of what Merton and indeed what Thomas Aquinas recognized to be the necessary link between the contemplative and active life. In so far as the Catholic schola can discover and develop that link between the contemplative and active life, they will be doing a great service, first of all to themselves, thereby making a significant contribution to evangelization in the Church and the world.

DISCUSSION GROUP FOUR:
NEW FORMS OF MINISTRY

James A. Coriden, Reporter

The group accepted a slogan which we thought summed up or characterized ministry as we had discussed it: "All ministry is collaborative." By this the group seemed to mean that in our day particularly cooperation and coordination of various efforts were right at the heart of developing ministry.

A. The group requests that the participants in the conference return to their educational institutions and place ministry squarely on the agenda of that college or university. The commitment to cooperation in ministry should be shared with those whom we represent. It is a common enterprise of the highest importance for the church in our day.

B. Some specific problems, projects, or programs which we feel need attention:

1. That the institutions create and the bishops fund in a major way the highest quality possible presentations for the mass media to present the underlying values which shape the change in our Church. There is a need to use the very best in the widest areas of communications to help shape the attitudes of our people and of our fellow citizens.

2. That training centers for various kinds of team ministries be devised and put into operation.

3. That the sense of the term "vocation," be redefined, perhaps by means of a special pastoral letter, so that it would include

ministry in its fullest breadth, the call which the leaders in the Church must extend to all of those who are ministering in so many ways within the Community of Faith.

4. That colleges attempt to have students involved in local parishes, perhaps by means of pairing or twinning a college with a local parish, thus providing both involvement and field experience as well as genuine pastoral assistance in the local community.

5. That a conscious attempt be made to insert an ethical component in the instruction in various disciplines, so that values might be examined and transmitted in our educational processes.

6. That existing centers of research and investigation be assessed and compared to the style of research institute which Dr. Noonan presented to the conference, e.g., the Woodstock Center for Theological Reflection in Washington.

7. That formation programs for effective campus ministry are in great need and should be formed.

8. That there is a special need for continuing education in theology for the laity, expecially those who are non-parents and who require a continual updating in their theological understanding.

9. That the consultation preceding the issuance of pastoral letters continue in a thoroughgoing way, with the recent examples of the pastoral on moral values and the Catechetical Directory showing us possible methods.

10. That there is urgent need for thoroughgoing catechesis on the new rite of penance.

11. That means be sought to evaluate ministries; that is, that our institutions help to design ways of measuring competence and success for those in ministry.

12. That all of us continue the efforts, so well begun here, to dissipate conflict and tension between hierarchy and academe, and that we seek to structure communications and collaboration so as to reduce hostility and promote ongoing cooperation. There is need for relational structures, and special sensitive listening in this process, particularly to women and young people

C. How these programs and projects are to be carried out might be the suitable subject for several conferences. There is obvious need for further study to specify and find out ways of solving particular problems. But, perhaps most important, is that leaders of Church and education be in continual dialogue; that ministry and school be involved reciprocally in addressing these ministerial needs. This is more than a mere methodology; it will shape and determine what we think about ministry and what we're doing in ministry. This close collaboration is the very heart of the matter.

DISCUSSION GROUP FIVE:
ECONOMIC CONCERNS

Leo V. Ryan, C.S.V., Reporter

The study group on economics concerns offers these six recommendations to the conference:

1. We recognize a changing economic order and recommend that we as Catholics, both the bishops and the academic community, be constructive critics of the economic system and be concerned that our scholarship and research seek to influence changes in the system in order to reflect values drawn from our Catholic heritage and tradition. We recognize in a very special way that form, structures, and the viability of our institutions are closely related to the economic system.

2. We recommend that scholars, in pursuing research in the economic fields, give a priority to researching the impact of American economic policy, both public and private in terms of the needs of the whole human community.

3. We recommend that bishops and scholars examine the issues and priorities which are emerging from the "Liberty and Justice for All" Bicentennial Program of the church, many of which appear to be economic issues of domestic and international concern; and, further, we encourage research in those issues and priorities as an occasion for the collaboration between the academic community and the hierarchy.

4. We are concerned especially with a proper recognition of the economic rights of women, aware that such a recognition calls also for an examination of the advantages and disadvantages such rights could bring to the family.

5. We declare our hope that the institutional Church in the United

States will use its resources and influence to foster the development of scholars, committed to their disciplines, who will serve the Church and the broader human community by the competent exercise of those disciplines.

6. We recommend that in the inquiries made by the Holy See, in seeking and examining candidates for the episcopacy, a question be included regarding the candidate's appreciation of the role of scholars and his willingness to collaborate with scholars, to seek their counsel in matters of concern in the Church; also, his own sensitivity to the need to do so in his pastoral ministry; we further recommend that scholars, college and university administrators, be encouraged to be aware of their responsibilities to assist the local Church in its need for scholarly input.

DISCUSSION GROUP SIX: PUBLIC POLICY QUESTIONS

J. Bryan Hehir, Reporter

Our comments really fall in two parts, because at first we explicitly kept the discussion on substantive matters and did not talk about specific projects. In terms of the substantive discussion, Bishop Dosier said he had a major issue of public policy on which he would like the group's reflections. And that was, that the Holy See was coming out on Thursday with a document on sexuality, and he knew that Thursday afternoon, in Memphis, somebody would be on the phone asking him what he thought about it, and he would like the reflections of the group. Actually the case study, if you would call it that, then raised several questions about the Church and public policy issues. For example, how is the Church perceived in public policy; what are regarded as really important issues in the Church on public policy; and why is it that whenever we speak on sexuality, we get the front page, and no matter what else we speak on, we're lucky if we get any space in the newspaper. The point was made, in fact, that what makes news is atypical responses: the Catholic community's response to sexual issues is different from the wider society, and therefore it is news. That was regarded as a very serious question, and not proposed humorously.

Secondly, in that same discussion, a question was raised about the content of our statements in the Church. That is to say, on sexual issues we tend to be very specific, very precise, and in fact do project a very distinct image vis-à-vis general cultural trends. When we speak on other social questions (at least the point was made in the group) the language is less precise, the stance is less stark, and we don't stand out so much against the dominant social trends.

Thirdly, the question of the credibility in Church statements as they affect the larger Church community.

These were the points discussed regarding the substance and style of the Church's teaching authority, relating to issues of public policy. Is there a distinct style of teaching authority when the Church moves into the areas of contingent policy discussion? Can the bishops take a stand on questions and yet make it clear that because the issue is contingent and the data is changing that the nature of the response from the larger community should be in the form of debate about those statements, rather than treat them as definitive? The final point raised about the teaching authority was simply an empirical point. It must be helpful if through the resources of universities, or other research institutes, we had a clearer sense today, ten years after the Council, seven years after *Humanae Vitae,* what in fact is the empirical state of affairs in the Catholic community regarding the credibility of the teaching authority of the Church?

Subsequent discussions were on projects which are listed here. First, this kind of forum should be continued on a regional basis. That statement was made more than once, and in fact we had two bishops from California in our group, as well as representatives from two colleges from California, and there has already been a decision made to hold a regional conference in California very similar to this conference, bringing together academicians and bishops. Secondly, there should be other forums created where this kind of discussion could take place. I think the sense of the meeting was, that apart from the specific issues discussed, the nature of this kind of interchange is so helpful to all parties concerned, that other forums ought to allow other members of the academic community to enter into this discussion.

Third, the National Catechetical Directory, and the specific relationship of the Church and public policy issues as it is found in that directory. Monsignor Paradis made the point that they have had more than 76,000 responses to the first draft of the Catechetical Directory, and one of the questions that surfaces very clearly is that there is major debate whether justice is the concern of the Church. He summarized some of the responses as people saying that we are obliged to do works of mercy and charity, but if there are any obligations in justice it is because we are citizens of the state, not because we are members of the Christian community. Monsignor Paradis made a strong pitch that a catechetical dimension is necessary if the mature community is to respond to policy statements.

Finally, specific areas where universities could contribute, and do contribute already to the public policy questions of the Church: 1) Research contracts: the universities generally service other sectors of society through research contracts, and there was a discussion about how, for example, the USCC could use the universities on that basis. 2) The Inter-University Committee on Research and Policy Studies, formed within the last year, is already cataloging the people doing research in the Catholic academic community across the United States, who have expressed an interest in offering their research to the Church, and whose material will be available soon. 3) Diocesan-funded research is not new in the Church; in fact Notre Dame has done a fair amount already. There is a history of that work and here are some existing models for the proposals we have heard tonight. 4) One of the specific areas that Catholic colleges and universities look to is the process of continuing education with different sectors of the Church. Very specifically, what about linking up with the unions in terms of their providing continuing education opportunities for their members, many of whom are Catholic? Also, continuing education for bishops and the clergy. One final point: one of our members felt strongly enough to say that just as after the war in France, the working man by and large was lost to the Church, so students are being lost to the Church today and that the first evangelizing task of the universities is precisely the people who are present with them every day.

Research Coordination in the American Church
George F. McLean, O.M.I.

Of the three roles of the college and university, namely, teaching, research, and service, this meeting has been concerned principally with ways in which the Catholic college can be of service to the Church. As a prelude to considering instruments of collaboration for service, the following notes describe what has been done in establishing a means of collaboration in another area—that of research.

THE PROBLEM

The context for recent developments in Catholic universities regarding research lies in the shift of attitude from the search for autonomy and academic freedom in the late sixties to the question articulated at the meeting of the International Federation of Catholic Universities at Salamanca in 1973: "How can we as scholars, colleges, and universities, working together, contribute to the life of the Church?"

The new question both implies and reveals a situation which differs crucially from that of Pére Lagrange, in whose day there existed, outside the Church, a developed body of scientific biblical scholarship, using anthropology, philology, and hermeneutics. Because of the anti-modernist reaction, this work had not been used by Catholic scholars. The task of Lagrange, therefore, was basically one of cautious assimilation—profound though the implications of that assimilation might be.

Today, on the contrary, Catholic scholars are very much in the mainstream and there is need to apply their capabilities to the content of the Christian tradition. This is a necessary condition for employing this tradition effectively in the effort by the Christian community today to understand its own life and its mission in the world. In turn, it implies bringing to the needs of the Church and of the total community the extensive research energies developed and supported by the Christian spiritual and material patrimony.

THE INTER-UNIVERSITY COMMITTEE ON RESEARCH AND POLICY STUDIES (ICR)

To the above purpose, in May 1975, Dr. Clarence C. Walton of the Catholic University of America invited the presidents and representatives of the U.S. member universities of the International Federation to discuss these needs and the means for a response. Four needs were identified: first, inquiry directed at self-understanding by the Christian community in its present stage of cultural development and in its concrete social articulation; second, exchange of information and ideas concerning the pastoral and social concerns of the Church; third, procedures for identifying thematic priorities and developing the needed research; and fourth, the location of relevant research capabilities and resources at the universities and in the larger intellectual community.

In answer to these needs, on May 14 the representatives decided to proceed as a group to form the Inter-University Committee on Research and Policy Studies in order to promote research efforts by U.S. Catholic scholars, universities, and other institutions by: (a) developing and maintaining an inventory of interested specialists and research capabilities in the various institutions and fields; (b) aiding in the process of identifying themes, concerns or problem areas; and (c) promoting the conditions in which interested scholars and institutions design and implement projects. The ICR Secretariate is presently located at the Catholic University of America.

The work of the ICR during the fall of 1975 has been twofold: the design of an inventory of scholars and of colloquia to define issues.

(a) Dr. Charles Dechert has designed an inventory of scholars with computer access by name, field of specialization, and diocese. Field tests at Catholic University, Purdue, and Mount St. Mary's show that this will engage 20–30% of the faculty, of the highest quality and from all fields, and that it will do so in response to an explicit invitation to place their capabilities at the service of the Church. A printout of the inventory by diocese will provide each bishop with a list of interested specialists to whom he can turn in his diocese or region; it will be available for use by the ICR, individual scholars, by the NCCB, and other interested parties in searching out needed capabilities for interdisciplinary projects.

(b) The colloquia have been designed as a means, not for doing research, but for identifying those precise topics which can make a difference for the realization of the Christian life and mission in our day.

What are the present needs? First, people: To engage scholars in this work is the purpose of the Committee, and field tests show that people can be found in significant numbers and in every area of specialization. The importance of this fact can hardly be overemphasized in the light of the major theme of Vatican II, namely, that the Church can be Christ living in the world only if it is constituted collegially. To realize this in the realm of scholarship implies the development, not of a few researchers whose conclusions others simply respect, but of a broad professional corps of active inquirers, searching each in his own way and in his own field for the meaning and the progress of God's creative work in our time. Second, Research topics: these are not lacking (see below), though the crucial and often underlying issues must be located precisely. Third, funds: As nothing comes from nothing, it is important to realistically assess the financial needs and include them in our priorities, for an inadequately financed project will inevitably fail—and then be cited as a precedent to discourage further effort. In the present case what is needed is not great, but the need is serious and present.

THE JOINT COMMITTEE OF LEARNED SOCIETIES AND SCHOLARS (CLS)

The development of the interuniversity project took place subsequent to an analogous step by the Catholic learned societies such as the American Catholic Philosophical Association, the Catholic Theological Society of America and others. Previously, these had been unrelated both (among) themselves and to the Church. After preliminary meetings with the NCCB, eight such societies established the Joint Committee of Catholic Learned Societies and Scholars in January 1975, with Donald Heintschel of the Canon Law Society as chairman.

The purposes of the Joint Committee are: First, to establish a cooperative effort and promote an attitude of mutual confidence between Catholic scholars and all parts of the Christian community; second, to provide a means of communicating information and ideas from the scholarly community to the bishops on matters of concern to their work in the Church; third, to receive indications from the National Conference of Catholic Bishops and to implement areas of scholarly work needed by the Church on the many levels of its pastoral work; and fourth, to carry out, on the part of the societies and scholars themselves, work needed in order to understand and respond to problems in contemporary Christian life.

Work during the spring focused upon aiding the ad hoc Bishops' Committee on Moral Values. This included a mail consultation which identified a dozen crucial issues, the preparation of a 150 page book of background memoranda, and a two-day meeting with the committee, during which an intensive, and self-corrective, dialogue took place between scholars and with the bishops. Future projects should provide time for doing in-depth background research.

Three CLS subcommittees have been planned corresponding to the threefold division of the research agenda described in the paper of Bishop Rausch. They will review research suggestions received from the NCCB (see below) and in the light of the content of the sciences establish a research agenda and priorities. An ad hoc committee will work on a white paper on scholarship in the Church.

FUTURE PROSPECTS

Through the interuniversity and the Learned Societies committees, universities, colleges and scholars have a structure for developing an active concern for, and engagement in, research needed by the Christian community. In time—if not immediately as by spontaneous generation—it should be possible to develop an intellectually vibrant scientific search for the broad Christian meaning of life. There is no reason why this cannot rival the intensive study of Thomas Aquinas in the Catholic community which was initiated by Leo XIII and which, after a number of decades, provided the fertile ground which gave birth to a number of outstanding efforts. From it came Étienne Gilson with his Institute of Medieval Studies, to which John Noonan has referred above, and which has made such a significant contribution. From it, too, has come Jacques Maritain for whom the university context made it possible to work out the implications of that vision for all phases of life. Finally, note should be made of Joseph Marechal whose progeny in the international system of Catholic higher education include Karl Rahner in Germany and Bernard Lonergan in Canada, with all their work has meant for the Church in the last 15 years.

The work of research in the Church has, indeed, a long and distinguished history. It challenges and encourages each generation to add its chapter. The above structures have been developed in our time to serve in this work, of which the present meeting is so fitting a consecration and proclamation.

Implementing Areas of Collaboration

Msgr. John F. Murphy

Because of the importance of the Borders' Committee in the new relationships between bishops on the one hand and Catholic college and university presidents on the other, it should be mentioned that the credit goes first of all to Cardinal Garrone who suggested its establishment; and then to Bishop Rausch and Archbishop Borders, who have very successfully communicated to presidents of colleges and universities around the country their really sincere interest in sharing with us the whole discussion of cooperation for the service of the Church. To them is due this credit and, although what we have done here for these few days moves us forward another step, we should not overlook the importance of the work of those who have met in the Borders' Committee over the last eighteen months.

It is lamentable that the meeting and the symposium which we have had here at Notre Dame for the last two days has been held in 1976 instead of 1950 or 1940 or 1930, but we cannot turn back the clock. We can only look to the future. We have spent two days in exploring the relationship the academic community and the Church, particularly the bishops, can have together. If we go away and leave it at the level of discussion, nothing will happen. Perhaps we are moving into the most important part of the program now in asking, what kind of mechanism, what kinds of devices, should we project to insure that what has been started here will continue. The organizers of this symposium have suggested that we spend the last portion of this final session talking about instruments of collaboration. All of you are asked to make whatever contribution you may have that will be of advantage in setting up such instruments of collaboration, and your suggestions may either be specific—as we would hope—or general.

Bishop Law: Two specific suggestions: One—I do not propose a model but I propose the problem—to draw into the kind of collaborative effort in behalf of the Church, those scholars, academicians who are Catholic but who are in institutions of higher learning which are not Catholic. Secondly, as a rather modest proposal, to continue the type of experience that we have had here, the Nieman Fellowship Program at Harvard for journalists could offer something of a model, where a setting would be provided for a group of bishops, college and university administrators, rectors of seminaries, academicians, to come together for a period of a month and simply interact. There would be no further agenda than that, and no greater expectation. The interaction of this group would bear its own fruit in terms of their future work, insights, and attitudes of mind and approach. I would suggest that such a plan would be a good way to further and intensify the kind of experience we have all enjoyed, and give the opportunity to others. Finally, just a very personal word of profound gratitude to everyone here, particularly those who planned it. I looked forward to this meeting very much. It really has exceeded my expectations in the hope that it has engendered in me and in the great confidence we must have in the people who are involved in academia for the Church.

Archbishop Borders: I would like to express the same gratitude as Bishop Law to the community of Notre Dame for hosting this meeting. Monsignor Murphy has requested responses as to how we can go beyond our present position; this is not an easy question to answer. Bishop Law made an excellent suggestion so far as growth and depth of individuals who probably later would make a contribution to the Church, but we do not have an implementing structure. This meeting represents an invitation from the University of Notre Dame, certainly with the collaboration of the ad hoc committee of college presidents and bishops. Everything that we have accomplished is going to be published, and I hope the book will be disseminated throughout the country both to the academic community and to the bishops.

Who is going to accept some responsibility for taking another step? I think there are only about three approaches which could be used: (1) The University and College Department of the NCEA might accept the challenge and offer some positive suggestions because they do have the contacts. (2) Certainly the Education Committee and the Education Department of the USCC have contacts with the bishops throughout the country. (3) Possibly Bishop McManus might again accept a challenge to establish a contact for future effort.

I would like also to express the hope that in any future consultations the seminary rectors and faculties be included. That is a dimension we probably all have missed during this present gathering, and a dimension we all need. Now moving from a position without any future structure, how are we going to implement what we have projected? I really think we have accomplished a great deal. We have discovered that all of us are relatively human, that we can listen to each other, and even relax with each other, like each other, and probably probe the conscience of each other. But we need to move forward to influence the country and provide an opportunity for growth. I hope that the avenues I have suggested will be at least examined by those in a position to accept this responsibility.

Father John Padburg: I want to thank Archbishop Borders for the suggestion he made. First, because obviously so many of our seminarians, rather than the old system of philosophy and theology, are getting a collegiate education, sometimes in their own colleges, seminary colleges, sometimes in other Catholic colleges. Secondly, because in many instances theological education is taking place on university campuses today and for the future, more importantly. It has taken us a fair amount of time to get together in a meeting such as this one. For the future, if some of us know each other better through the course of years, as bishops, as administrators, as educators, as pastors, it might not take so long.

Father Philip Murnion: I want to mention that there is another group missing, as it were; that is, people who do not represent either office or expertise but who have surfaced as being popularly representative of constituencies in the Church. For example, the absence of any Hispanic people in this group would have been remedied to some extent if there were ways of surfacing people who have become sort of natural leaders of their people. If is difficult to locate such people because we do not have widespread vehicles; we do not have a national association of the laity that might have emerged as a way of fostering that leadership. Nonetheless the people seem to me to be the third part of the triangle we are trying to work out, namely, the official leadership in the Church, professional leadership in the Church, and popularly-elected leadership

111

in the Church. We need all three poles present, it seems to me, if we will not have both the professionals and the bishops asserting their representativeness of that group in ways that perhaps exceed the reality. I would urge that some way be found for introducing that element more formally into the discussions.

Father Burell: One of the things we have noticed here is that here are two needs which can roughly be summarized as research and service. We have in the committee that George McLain has reported on, The Inter-University Research Committee, an instrumentality for coordinating research; and the NCEA would be an appropriate instrumentality for setting up a standing committee to monitor initiatives for service for Catholic colleges in dioceses. So I would propose sharing the seed money that is ear-marked for ongoing initiatives from this conference equally between those two groups.

Bishop Rausch: I want to say something personally and then something as General Secretary. Very personally, I want to say that this is the beginning of the unfolding of a dream, and for me it has been a tremendous inspiration to be here with all of you these days. Institutionally, I want to say that if the office of the General Secretary can in any way be supportive in the future, I will certainly try to do all that I can. I feel it is an honor that the Bishops Conference was able to be involved, as it was, in the planning and participation and execution of this meeting.

Monsignor Murphy: I think it is incumbent upon me to speak on your behalf, a formal word for the record of deepest appreciation to Notre Dame. I represent, in the job I have in Washington, all of the Catholic universities and colleges in the country, and all of them are dear to me, all of them are in the service of the Church, all of them are in the service of the country. They must all be treasured and nutured. On their behalf, I am grateful for the kinds of support that have been expressed, the expressions of support made also by those of you who do not come from Catholic institutions, and the kinds of encouragement you have all given in the course of this meeting.

But I think that we owe something special to Notre Dame. There is no institution in the country which more quickly responds to the spoken and even unspoken needs of the Church. It has a long record, and I think all of us should acknowledge the kind of national leadership which Notre Dame takes on behalf of the Church. It is a great university which serves the country, but in a special way it is a great university which serves the Church. It displays great loyalty in this service, as is shown by the symposium offered here to the American Church. To Father Hesburgh we owe one more vote of thanks added to the many votes of thanks that we have owed him, and I hope have given him over the years.

A new thing has happened in the American Church, and in the American colleges and universities since I have been privileged to be associated with them, a period of over twenty-five years. In the place of suspicion or indifference or tension, there has been visible, among bishops, in particular, and college and university presidents, a new interest, a new trust, a new openness, a new willingness to explore together, new ways in which to serve the country and the people of God. If I can speak on behalf of the colleges and universities, I would encourage all of you to probe with us, to push us, to needle us, to ask us constantly, what have we done for you this week. The Catholic college or university, in no way diminishing its academic function and role, is able to give a very special kind of service to the Church, and is open and willing and anxious to provide this service. What we have done here in the last two days is prelude to something greater for the future. So, instead of ending a conference by saying, thank you, this is ended; I should think we would say: thank you for coming; let us now begin.

V. REFLECTIONS ON THE SYMPOSIUM: ITS PROCESSES AND GOALS

Commentary
Richard W. Conklin

It was fitting that the movement of Catholic educators and bishops "from détente to entente" (to use Archbishop Bernardin's phrase) took place at Notre Dame, for the university and its president, Father Theodore M. Hesburgh, were both involved at the very beginning of the dialogue the Evangelization Conference intended to further.

The conference lasted three days but was almost a decade in the making. Its history can be traced back to 1967 when a group of North American Catholic educators issued the so-called "Land-O-Lakes Statement" from a Notre Dame seminar center in Wisconsin. The statement asserted the autonomy of Catholic colleges and universities and affirmed academic freedom in the sensitive area of theological scholarship. It put forth as an educational model the kind of Catholic institution of higher learning commonly found in the United States—a college or university not erected by canon law but chartered by civil statute, one in the service of the Church but not governed by it.

From 1967 to 1972, the International Federation of Catholic Universities carried on a worldwide dialogue with the Vatican about the nature of a contemporary Catholic institution of higher learning, finally obtaining in 1973 a somewhat reserved but nonetheless important legitimation from the Sacred Congregation for Catholic Education, headed by Cardinal Gabriel Garrone.

Having made their point about independence, Catholic educators decided the next step was to talk about interdependence. The purpose of the Notre Dame meeting with its theme of "Evangelization in the American Context" was to bring the discussion to a new level, one which explored how American Catholic colleges and universities could help the Church in its mission.

Those who thought that the tension between the Church's teaching authority and the freedom necessary for research and scholarship had been resolved, however, were mildly surprised by the keynote address by Archbishop Joseph L. Bernardin, president of the National Conference of Catholic Bishops. In a talk both irenic and optimistic, Archbishop Bernardin nonetheless managed to use the words "magisterium" or "magisteria" two dozen times in 19 pages, casting the shadow of old debates over what was intended to be a forward-looking collaboration.

Later in the conference, Jesuit Father William Sullivan, provost of Seattle University, wondered aloud whether the three-year-old agreement on the nature of Catholic higher education was not being compromised by Vatican officials still unable to understand how any school could call itself Catholic without a juridical tie to Rome. He referred to recent communications between Cardinal Garrone and American bishops and educators which seem to imply that Rome made no distinction between colleges and universities on the one hand and seminaries on the other, a distinctly pre-1973 curial mind-set. Sullivan called on U.S. bishops to defend Catholic educational institutions against their critics both foreign and domestic.

While the memory of old ideological estrangement lingered, the sharp cleavage between bishops and educators anticipated by some simply was not evident, even in the candid give and take of the conference's small group sessions. Those sessions ranged widely from "new ministry" to "Catholic identity" in an attempt to chart some courses for a shared approach to problems besetting the American church. It was the first time most bishops and educators had sat down at the same table and discussed shared concerns, and, although outnumbered, the hierarchy held its own in seminar banter.

It was evident to this observer, however, that some basic problems of definition exist. It is still difficult for bishops to grasp the curious nature of the academic enterprise, one which insists on freedom for inquiry and reflection but stops short of full commitment on particular social issues. "Where were the Catholic colleges and universities when the bishops were out front on the farm labor problem?" asked one bishop in a seminar session. A question more to the point would be how far "out front" any educational institution can be on any given moral or social issue. The members of an academic community have all the freedom they need in the classroom and in the research situation, but the educational institution itself is limited by the necessity to guarantee unfettered commerce in ideas, even while, in the case of Church-related schools, maintaining a public religious commitment. One suspects that on gut issues—such as abortion—the nation's bishops are yearning to ask more than Catholic colleges and universities feel they can appropriately give—a formal institutional stand alongside the Church. Notre Dame, for example, has turned down requests that its board of trustees formally commit the university to an antiabortion position.

A distillation of the conference's background papers, major addresses, and small group discussion left three large areas of potential contribution to the church from Catholic educational institutions: teaching, research, and service. The first of these, which assumes, as Auxiliary Bishop John S. Cummins of Sacramento put it, a graduate who is "a man or woman of faith—cultivated, critical, and mature," might be assuming too much, according to some at the conference.

Indiscriminate faculty hiring, an influx of theologically illiterate students and the quest to enter the mainstream of American higher education over the last decade have severely weakened many institutions' sense of their own Catholic identity, according to some critics at the conference. While a few Catholic educators tacitly accepted such criticism, others were quick to argue that the trend was in the opposite direction as one school after another rearticulated what it meant educationally to stand in a religious tradition.

Perhaps the easiest point of contact between the institutional church and its universities loomed in the area of research. Several commentators pointed to areas such as the family, genetic ethics, and urban planning, where the Church's need for facts and their sophisticated interpretation could keep Catholic researchers busy for decades.

The problem is, legal scholar John Noonan noted, that only four percent of all American faculty members identify themselves as having heavy research interests, and the actual pool of research scholars thus available to the Church is even smaller.

Noonan advocated setting up specialized research institutes, composed of a small number of Catholic scholars engaged in full-time research in depth as a long-range response to the church's need for new knowledge.

In the area of service, continuing education was an oft-mentioned vehicle, especially valuable to the local Church. The training of lay persons to fill expanded roles in the Church—such as in religious education—now is being done by several Catholic educational institutions for their dioceses.

The NCEA is expected to assume the major burden of conference follow-up, and at least one regional conference (California) was proposed to continue the dialogue between Catholic educators and bishops.

(Whether the focus should be on local programs or whether some national coordination is needed drew a divided response from educators. Those who had been enjoying peaceful coexistence, or better, with their chanceries, thought a few local success stories would greatly benefit the idea of collaboration. Others, whom experience had made wary of local initiatives, preferred the push to come from Washington.)

In the area of research, the interuniversity committee on research and policy studies at Catholic University of America was already feeding an inventory of American Catholic scholars into a computer and stood in the best position to coordinate efforts in its area. The International Federation of Catholic Universities also announced the establishment of a research center in Paris.

The root question of the meeting—"can Catholic colleges and universities be places where the Church can comfortably do some of its thinking?"—received a tentative yes.

Ad Meipsum

Ralph M. McInerny

I was invited to the symposium in my guise as professor of philosophy with the ultimate task of writing up my impressions of what I saw and heard. During the three days I was often tempted to react as a novelist. Images if not scenarios pressed upon the mind: bearded theologians in pin stripe suits, a portly prelate resplendent in a red lumberjack shirt, so many nuns who looked like favorite aunts, a sprinkling of laity, jaded journalists. It would have been easy to coax a plot and theme from all that, but I was not really led into temptation. Fiction requires distance and I could not view these preceedings from some imaginative afar. As a philosopher, then, but not as Pythagoras saw the type, an observer of, not a participant in, the game of life. The others were, in the main, archbishops, bishops, clergy from the various bureaus, university and college administrators. No one's idea of an average crowd, certainly not constant companions of mine, and yet increasingly I felt at home with them. The reasons for this, as I reflect on them now, are personal but not, I think, merely private. One of Scott Fitzgerald's characters describes himself as that narrowest of specialists, the well-rounded man. Life, he concludes, is much better looked at from a single window after all. As with charity, we really have no choice. We are forbidden to judge others not because we could and shouldn't, but because we can't. So too we can only see things from our own window. Of course that does not prevent us from seeing what is there.

The point of the symposium, as I understand it, was to look for ways in which Catholic institutions of higher learning could be of help to the bishops in their task of evangelization. That might seem to be a quest for a relation between two somewhat abstract groupings. My own thoughts were drawn to one term of the relation, the university. Its spokesmen here were presidents and vice-presidents, but for whom would they speak? I confess that I found it somewhat strange to sit in various rooms in the Center for Continuing Education and find that the Catholic college or university was being regarded as a source on which the hierarchy might draw in order to achieve various ends. Strange, because it was difficult not to think how very odd many of my colleagues would find the underlying assumption. How many of us see our quotidian task as professor of this or that in any possible relation to the concerns of bishops? The fact is that over the years the faculty member of the Catholic college or university has come to see himself as indistinguishable in his concerns from his colleagues on the faculties of secular institutions. When this identification is not perfect, it is nonetheless before him as an ideal. How did this come about?

I am in my third decade of what have not always seemed the glorious mysteries of my tenure on the faculty of Notre Dame. It was still more or less the rule, back in 1954, for a Catholic layman to come into philosophy by way of the seminary. He was always, to a greater or lesser degree, a spoiled priest. The good side of this was that he saw his task as teacher in vocational terms. The use of his talents was seen in the light of a notion of the spiritual life he had picked up in seminary days. He found it quite natural to view his efforts as part of the work of the Church in the world. He found it equally natural to be a Thomist, and his reasons for this were drawn from the great encyclicals on the matter. In those days, the appeal of such a symposium as this would have arrived to willing ears. Things are different now. The milieu in which one works has altered. Even doubting Thomists are rare birds now. There has been an increase in the number of non-Catholics on our faculties. The question, "What is a Catholic university?" has been heard in the Land-O-Lakes and elsewhere. Many of my colleagues are genuinely puzzled, some even feel threatened, by this question. The Catholic university cannot be assumed to be a source readily disponible to episcopal needs.

It should be recognized that this changed situation on the campus is the direct result of our heeding earlier calls to action. Fifteen or so years ago, it suddenly became fashionable to ask a set of urgent questions. Where are our great institutions of higher learning? Where are our Catholic scientists and humanists, our writers and poets? Where are the Catholic political leaders one might have assumed would pour from our colleges? The implication of these questions was that something had gone grievously wrong. I think it fair to say that Notre Dame, under the presidency of Father Hesburgh, has led the way in the drive toward excellence in Catholic higher education. What was wanted was a place that would attract and foster talent with the result that the Catholic university would compare favorably with the best universities in the land. The ideal was one of supreme attraction. Who could resist the appeal to do excellently what he was already doing somehow? Who does not need the stimulus of such teleological goading and guiding? Here and elsewhere the effort began. It goes on today. The results are far from negligible. While stellar prominence in one's field is rare, it is not unknown, and the well-trained, respected faculty member is the rule. The graduate program in my own department is high in national rankings.

This academic excellence has been won, however, at the price of making the Catholic university, in its faculty, estranged from appeals like that of this symposium. New recruits to the faculty are drawn from the most promising candidates nationally available. They are not often Catholics. They come to Notre Dame because they do not perceive its Catholic character to be relevant to the job they are being hired to do. Once here, particularly if they have previously taught in secular universities, they are wont to speak of the spirit of the place, of its congenial atmosphere, but the merits they see are expressible in humanist terms and make little or no appeal to the religious. It is almost as if Catholic universities, having striven for excellence in order more effectively to function, thereby ceased being Catholic.

Needless to say, this was not the intended result. Administrators and boards of trustees did not set out to secularize the Catholic university. Most would question that this has indeed happened. All are concerned that academic excellence and a Catholic nature be twin characterizations of their university. Yet no one knows quite how to bring this about in the situation that has emerged. At the outset, I suspect, non-Catholic faculty were looked upon as adjuncts, as not quite full-fledged members of a basically Catholic faculty, much as, in an earlier time, the lay professor had status secondary to that of his clerical colleague, accepted as he was as a *pis aller* until vocations increased. But there is only one kind of faculty member once tenure has been achieved. And ultimately, certainly so far as the hopes of this symposium go, the Catholic college or university is its faculty. Administrators come and go, the student body turns over quadrennially, but a faculty is relatively stable, it assumes a character, it is, for better or worse, the true vehicle of the institution's history. I doubt that there are many faculties of Catholic colleges or universities that see themselves as potential instruments for the evangelization of American society.

Such thoughts might seem to dictate a cynical response to the symposium's meetings and addresses and discussions. Have I not suggested that in its effort to build a bridge between bishop and college, the symposium had a mistaken notion of one term of the hoped-for relation? But on every day of the symposium I was confronted by specific discussions, realistic hopes, actual cases of the aid scholarship and research can be to the bishops. It became clear that, if it is wrong to think of the Catholic university as a great monolith hungering to become involved in what we used to call Catholic Action, our campuses do contain many zealous and apostolic faculty members and dozens of pertinent programs; in short, what the symposium was after did not turn out to be as yet unrealized possibilities but the expansion and multiplication of existent actual instances of bridges between campus and bishop. John Noonan laid out a number of grandiose schemes for our consideration, and the very models he chose to illustrate what he was after showed that the thing can be done because it has been done. Michael Novak's group, discussing Catholic identity, kept coming back to the heterogeneousness of American Catholicism, the positive role of ethnic differences. How wrong to smooth away such differences in pursuit of some unexamined ideal of Americanization. Perhaps this suggests thoughts on the university.

Whatever the merit of our pursuit of academic excellence, and they are many, that pursuit began with an exaggeratedly negative estimate of what Catholic education had been. Moreover, it accepted too unquestioningly as normative a conception of academic excellence drawn from the paradigmatic institutions, chiefly of the Ivy League. Well, we have come to suspect that things were not all that excellent in our models. After all, they were the source of the Best and the Brightest. No Watergate footpad or scofflaw came from our campuses. Currently it is a national concern that the life of the mind not be divorced from wider and sustaining concerns, precisely the concerns which animate religious faith. How poignant that, in pursuing excellence, we played down, unwittingly, what had been the soul and spirit of our institutions.

Do not think that I am pointing back to a lost golden age. The Notre Dame I came to years ago was lots of things; it was neither as bright as it seems to the eye of nostalgia nor as bleak as the mindless progressive imagines. Like the Church herself in the Fifties it contained both good and bad. In any case, the line of time is forward and we are where we are. In the present setting the old spirit, the Catholic spirit, is still alive. It may be in diaspora, but is that wholly bad? On an analogous point, I am convinced that Thomism is healthier today when there are fewer

Thomists. Perhaps something like that is true of Catholics on our faculties.

My remarks are finally *ad meipsum*. I came to the symposium as a species of observer. Perhaps I dreamt of casting a cold judgmental eye of the proceedings. I found an occasion for self-examination. It seems wrong to ask if the faculties of our schools are such as to respond to the appeal of this symposium. The appeal works subtly on its addressees. It is an old adage that *amicitia pares aut invenit aut facit*. Maybe appeals fashion rather than simply find their hearers. I found myself stirred anew by a sense of vocation, welcomed the thought that what I do as a philosopher can have a further significance in the work of the Church. I was shamed to realize that I had lost that sense, at least to some degree. Not every ear is an itching ear, in the Pauline sense. Significantly, perhaps, it is the Douay version that echoes in my mind. In his Book of Problems, Aristotle asks why we like the old songs best. Some Golden Oldies replayed themselves in my mind during these three days, but I suspect that the arrangements were different, the beat newer, some of the words unusual. Who in the old days would have spoken of evangelization? I ended with the conviction that this symposium is a way to redefine two shores as well as to throw a bridge between them.

A Conversation Begins
Russell B. Shaw

The hubbub in the South Bend airport was exceptional for a
Sunday afternoon. Much of it was produced by Notre Dame
students, boys and girls, returning to campus from their
semester break, who thronged cheerfully around the bag-
gage retrieval area. Among them—but also somewhat
isolated—was a sprinkling of middle-aged persons, reserved by comparison with the students and distinguished,
some of them, by black suits and overcoats and Roman
collars. What impact, a new arrival asked himself, would it
make on the young people to know that these were leading
figures in the Catholic Church in the United States, gathering at Notre Dame for a conference on "evangelization in
the American context"? The question seemed to answer
itself.

Different people bring different expectations to a meeting. The symposium on evangelization in the American context was no exception.
There may have been half a dozen—or half a hundred—private agendas
on hand. Probably none of them was fully accomplished or fully disappointed.
The agendas least fulfilled were based on the assumption that the
discussion would deal heavily with evangelization as such—its nature,
its problems and opportunities, its methods and agents. Evangelization
did provide a legitimizing rubric, a way of fitting the dialogue into a
nonthreatening context. To be fair, it must also be said that what was
discussed pertains, in one way or another, to evangelizing. But it was
not evangelization itself. "Perhaps it was a mistake to use the word in
the title," one participant who had taken part in planning the meeting
remarked during a coffee break, when a certain formlessness was afflict-

ing the dialogue. "Really, we're here to talk about two other questions, and both are very important. Can the Catholic colleges and universities work together with the bishops? And if they can, how?"

Perhaps even the first question did not really need to be discussed. At least not by the hundred or so cooperation-minded people at this meeting. It was taken for granted that working together was possible and, more than possible, necessary. Archbishop Joseph Bernardin's comment in his opening paper—that the symposium marked a movement from détente to entente in the relations between bishops and the Catholic academic community—fell upon ears primed for just such a phrase-making summary of the state of the question.

Every meeting develops its own clichés. One of the favorites here, repeated in various ways, was, "We have enough topics for another dozen symposiums." This makes summing-up a difficult and necessarily subjective task. Still, certain themes did predominate.

> A professor at a large Catholic university: "Many of my colleagues would be surprised to know that a meeting like this was taking place and that the subject was how they could do more to be of service to the Church. I don't mean to be a pessimist, but I think we had better be a bit cautious in assuming that there is a large number of ready and willing collaborators out there."

One subject which received a great deal of attention was the "Catholic identity" of Catholic institutions of higher education. To a great extent it was considered in relation to the larger question of the Catholic identity of American Catholics. Michael Novak's background paper was devoted to "Catholic identity" question, as was one of the symposium workshops, which Novak also chaired—and whose participants agreed that they preferred to talk about "Catholic identities." In outline at least, the Novak thesis is fairly simple.

For many reasons, Catholics in the United States have historically not exercised, and do not now exercise, an influence on American political, economic and cultural life in proportion to their numbers. Furthermore, American Catholics in recent years have been considerably influenced by secularizing forces at work in American society generally. Catholics in growing numbers have certainly been moving into the mainstream of American life, but for many this has been at a price: the price of some measure of their Catholicity. It is possible, for instance, that many of the "bright young Catholic college graduates" of recent years have, knowingly or not, been co-opted into the service of cultural forces inimical to Catholic values.

A comparable development has been taking place in Catholic higher education, many agreed, with money as one catalyst. In many places (New York state is a notable example) Catholic institutions of higher education have been under strong and continuing pressure to reduce or abandon their specifically "Catholic" identity as a condition for receiving public funds. For better or worse, this has coincided with the post-Vatican II turmoil in the Church and with speculation (or more) among Catholic academicians about the desirability of putting distance between their institutions and ecclesiastical authority. To complicate matters further, some Catholic colleges and universities, pursuing academic excellence, have in the past fifteen years or so hired faculty with little or no regard for the religious or ideological orientation of those hired.

Such considerations did not cast a pall over the symposium. They did come to the surface, however, whenever talk about enlisting Catholic academicians in the direct service of the Church seemed to envision this as an easy, almost effortless process. Unquestionably many faculty members at Catholic schools are both qualified and willing to place their talents at the service of the Church, locally or nationally. An effort to inventory Catholic faculties in order to identify such persons appears already to have located a substantial number. Yet the negative point remained uncontested: there are many who would just not be interested. Perhaps the answer is simply to move ahead with collaborative ventures—to begin to develop projects in which the assistance of Catholic teachers and scholars is needed and wanted—and trust that many of them will get on board when they see that there is a vehicle at hand to accommodate them.

> Lay participant: "I'm a little uneasy about the fact that the people here keep talking about the bishops as 'pastors.' I suppose it isn't intended, but there seems to be a kind of implicit depreciation of the teaching authority of bishops."

> Bishop participant: "That hasn't struck me. I've always thought that to be a pastor means to be a teacher—among other things."

The commentary on the symposium by Richard Conklin took note of the fact that, in a "most irenic and optimistic" keynote address of nineteen typed pages, Archbishop Bernardin of Cincinnati, President of the National Conference of Catholic Bishops and the United States Catholic Conference, used the words magisterium and magisteria two dozen times. The statistic made a point. Some of the symposium participants wished to discuss directly the relationship of Catholic scholars to the teaching authority of the Church; but some did not.

Both attitudes are understandable. The view of those who did not wish directly to discuss the question might perhaps be summarized this way: this matter has often been a bone of contention between bishops and scholars in recent years; reopening the question now would reopen old wounds and cause new controversies; we are better advised to put this question aside and get on with the practical work of collaboration; in doing so, the automony of Catholic scholarship should be taken for granted. As for the viewpoint of those who want to discuss the question, perhaps it goes something like this: granted the desirability of avoiding needless quarrels and getting on with the work of collaboration, the question is still work discussing; discussion doesn't rule out collaboration—on the contrary, if it is done reasonably and responsibly, it can help put collaboration on a firmer footing; the idea is not to destroy the autonomy of Catholic scholarship, it is to get a clearer understanding of what autonomy means in a unique body like the Catholic Church.

The result at Notre Dame was something of a standoff. Those like Archbishop Bernardin, who wished to discuss the question, raised it periodically. Those who did not wish to discuss it let it pass. (Perhaps also one should note a third group, somewhat overlapping one or both of the others, made up of those who are uneasy about Rome's intentions toward Catholic colleges and universities and wish assurances of episcopal support.)

This does not mean that the relationship of the bishops and the academicians went unexamined at Notre Dame. But the examination was for the most part more pragmatic than theoretical: how can we help each other?

> In the United States in 1974, 6.6 million Catholic children of elementary and secondary school age were not receiving formal religious education, either in Catholic schools or out-of-school programs. This was an increase of 3.5 million— more than 100%—over the figure of 3.1 million in 1965. (Statistics from *Where Are the 6.6 Million?*, a report prepared by the Office of Research, Policy and Program

Development, Department of Education, United States
Catholic Conference).

What can Catholic colleges and universities do by way of more direct
involvement in the mission of the Church? Apart from the primary role
of teaching, two other functions stood out in the Notre Dame discussions: research and service.

John Noonan's paper on research made a strong impact on the meeting. Using the models of Catholic biblical scholarship and the institutes
of Étienne Gilson and Stephan Kuttner, he argued for a well funded
research center, staffed by a small number of scholars, in which serious
longterm research would be carried on in areas of concern to the
Church. Although stimulating, Professor Noonan's proposal was felt by
some symposium participants to have problematical aspects, particularly in apparently dismissing efforts to involve relatively large numbers
of Catholic scholars in some form of "research" on behalf of the
Church nationally and locally.

Whatever the future of the Noonan plan, other potentially important
things are now happening in this area, and they provide a significant
part of the background for what happened at Notre Dame. The inventory
of Catholic faculty members, mentioned earlier, is one. The consultative participation of scholars (including a June 1975, seminar in Washington, D.C., organized by the Joint Committee of Catholic Learned
Societies) in the work of preparing a bishops' collective pastoral letter
on moral values is another. The same group's successful effort to elicit
suggestions from senior staff of the bishops' conference with respect to
issues and priorities in research and its subsequent creation of subcommittees to pursue these, is a third. Clearly the entire enterprise is tentative at this stage and still finding its way, but perhaps what is most
important about it is that it has begun.

With respect to service, much of the discussion concerned various
forms of continuing education, field education, and so forth. The principal emphasis here was on service to the local church, including
parishes in the vicinity of particular institutions. Several bishops, however, noted that "service" in this context should not be thought of
univocally, precisely because the needs and circumstances of small rural
dioceses are quite different from those of large urban dioceses, and the
differences must be taken seriously in shaping and delivering service
from the academic community to the local Church. One workshop
suggested accelerated development on Catholic campuses of centers for

the study, renewal, and practice of prayer and spirituality; these were seen not only as instruments of service to the larger Church, but as means for evangelizing the academic community itself.

A cautionary note, similar to that raised with respect to the attitudes of faculty members in Catholic institutions, was introduced concerning the institutional potential of existing Catholic schools. Professor Noonan, for example, in urging the creation of a Catholic law school committed to Catholic legal values and traditions, deplored the dominance of secular models in legal education. Evelyn Whitehead made a similar point in observing that the secular university model holds the field in the United States and provides the environment—negative in some ways, positive in others—within which Catholic institutions of higher education do in fact function.

> A staff member at a large Catholic university: "Frankly, most of the kids at my school are just indifferent toward the institutional Church. But after graduation many of them go through a kind of reentry process as far as the Church is concerned, especially after they marry and begin to have kids of their own. Then they confront the question, 'Do I want my own children to grow up as pagans?' Usually the answer is no."

The leadership of the Catholic Church in the United States (which is many more people than the bishops alone) has suffered a series of nasty shocks in recent years. Enumerating them would be tedious, unnecessary, and depressing. Words like "polarization," "confrontation," and "turned-off" have been the stock in trade for discussions of the state of the Church for some time; while the conditions to which they refer certainly do not exhaust the reality of Catholicism in this country, there is no doubt that they are part of it.

The relationship between Catholic higher education and the bishops is part of this picture. For the last ten years or so this relationship has been troubled and uncertain. There are many reasons. Perhaps one of the principal reasons is that those on each side expected more than those on the other were willing or able to deliver: on the bishops' side, responsive docility of the Catholic academic community to ecclesiastical authority; on the side of Catholic higher education, toleration if not approbation by the hierarchy for whatever the academicians wished to do in the name of their autonomy.

The Notre Dame symposium was a serious attempt to come to grips with this situation. Both its strengths and its weaknesses lay in its basically pragmatic orientation. Although serious questions were raised about the relationship of the magisterium to academic freedom and autonomy, they were not really discussed. Perhaps this is a momentary phenomenon. (How much, after all, can a hundred people accomplish in less than three days?) Perhaps, however, it represents a partial consensus that such questions had better *not* be discussed—at least, not now—if there is to be any realistic hope of cooperation between the bishops and the academicians. If the latter, arguments could be made both for and against the correctness of the approach.

How evaluate such a meeting? A journalist, sitting in the midst of his luggage in the lobby of the Morris Inn the morning after the symposium ended, said he was working up his notes for the piece he would write. "The lead is, 'The most important thing about this meeting is that it took place.' " That may have summed up the attitude of most of those who attended. The mere occurrence of a meeting—even so challenging and, in many ways, encouraging and even inspiring a meeting as this—does not justify enormous rejoicing. What is justified is modest satisfaction that an interrupted conversation has been begun again in tentative but civil tones; together with a more than modest hope that, as the conversation proceeds, it will become both more specific (in relation to projects) and more general (in relation to fundamental issues) than the conversation at Notre Dame was or possibly could have been.

Recommendations
Joseph Cunneen

I have no brilliant reflections on the symposium: probably college presidents and bishops are better judges of its usefulness. Most people I talked to thought of it as a useful first step, which can at this point only be translated into practicality on the local level. But there we are back to box one, since in general we can assume that (with some having genuine conflicts of schedule) the bishops most open and the Catholic scholars who are *not* the most alienated or anti-institution were the ones who came. I suspect the first meeting was just as well to leave rather open, without too definite an agenda, but my prejudice would be to have all parties considering rather more concrete proposals or substantial background reading; as it is, we took quite a while to establish vocabularies or know what the other person's problems were.

I would recommend that a subcommittee of Catholic university administrators and scholars (if they can work together; if not, two committees) should formulate a short statement, preferably with reference to some concrete examples, on what kinds of cooperation they would like from the bishops, what modes of consultation would be useful, and what kinds of service(s) they believe they (and their institutions) have to offer. (Without excluding the special contribution of Catholic institutions, more significant representation of Christian scholars in non-Catholic institutions is necessary if an unintentional ghetto spirit is to be avoided.) Similarly, the bishops should formulate a tentative statement of the various roles and services they would like to see Catholic institutions and scholars provide, specifically with a pastoral concern as at least ultimate justification. This could be supplemented by individual or regional requests—as brought home in my subpanel by a couple of attractively pastoral-minded bishops in rural localities with little in the way of Catholic educational institutions nearby.

With considerable awareness of the planning problems, the schedule conflicts, and the absence of a large enough pool of Catholic scholars in certain fields or representing certain groups, I always feel a sense of despair in going to meetings (academic, political, Catholic, or only social parties) that are lily-white. I know we can't produce the number of black sister college presidents we want overnight, but we have then got to compensate in one way or another by inviting scholars, activists, etc., since *we all* need constantly to hear the voices that our social history would otherwise remove from our consideration. (With the Spanish-speaking, it should be easier, even though we can't expect too many Puerto Rican John Noonans at this point.)

I would make two related recommendations. Why can't the bishops announce a theme for reflection on the part of Catholic scholars in 1977? e.g., poverty, work, death, male and female, reverence for life. . . . In fall '76 and winter '76–77, Catholic colleges and universities would sponsor whatever workshops, symposia, and other projects they thought appropriate for publicizing the national concern of the Church as a whole and what contribution the institution could make locally. In spring '77 more of same. In fall '77 a prestige-and-publicity two-or three-day meeting with invited speakers, held in a major city and/or in connection with a major Catholic university, with speakers familiar with papers and activities conducted during the year, and producing a quality paperback of the conference, which would be intended as a rough equivalent to the *Semaine des intellectuels catholiques*, held annually in France. A case could be made for reversing the order, having the "Semaine" prestige meeting in mid-winter '77, so that paperback with proceedings and bibliography could be a study volume for the whole Church at all Catholic colleges and Newman clubs for the year. The hope would be that the meetings and publicity and national discussion would not only dramatize that the Christian intelligence is active in the modern world, but that the process would also constitute a broad consultative process by the bishops with the Catholic community (obviously nonbinding) and that the bishops would issue a pastoral on the theme at their spring meeting in '78. What is good about this, apart from possibly a healthy boost to elan and publicizing of Christian thought, is that it doesn't require large foundation support, although I assume the host Catholic university could get such support for its meeting on the national level. The local college meetings should mostly use local resources and be self-supporting.

The above may be a side-alley from the main lines of development of the Notre Dame meeting, but it strikes me as one that would in part cure the inevitable co-optation of Catholic intellectualism by the strong forces of success-building and secularism in U.S. university life (alas, not only in secular universities). My other point is that, in follow-up meetings, the occasion be used more consciously to broaden our horizons. The immediate agenda that is apt to be brought up by both bishops and invited Catholic academics may mire us in the past, or at the very least prevent us from being useful to the pastoral scene of 2000 that is fast upon us. The bishops are apt to have a wiser and more concerned eye for the difficulty of reaching these teenagers in these parishes, but we all need to prepare for the kind of world these kids will live in. My constant refrain is that Catholics aren't very catholic, which is especially crazy now that even in the U.S. all the great spiritualities of the world are already being practiced at a serious level (along with even more quackery) and that there is no way for the options of a Notre Dame undergraduate to be seen by him in the way they were by you or me (was it that long ago?).

VI. BACKGROUND PAPERS

The Catholic College in the Catholic Community

Most Rev. John S. Cummins

Catholic colleges share with bishops today a joint responsibility in the contemporary social mission of the Church. To the wider Catholic community the colleges continue their traditional educational contribution.

These are the two issues which I wish to address in this paper.

By way of preliminary, I will attempt to make explicit my own appreciation of the relationship of the universities to Church authority. I believe my posture on this lively question will have some bearing on the reflections to follow.

I

With regard to the relationship of higher education to Church authority, whatever battles have taken place in the past, the autonomy of the university seems to me a question clearly decided. The university, however, both by its tradition and its declaration of purpose exists as part of the community of the Church. There is a relationship that can be described, I believe, in terms of mutuality existing between the university and other elements of the community including the hierarchy. The university will benefit from the conscious and active support of the Catholic community, including clergy. On the other hand, it will find detrimental any opposition or hostility from them.

As part of the community, the university will have both the opportunity and the obligation to serve that community. Too much consciousness, however, of service to the local Church can affect the educational mission of the university. The apologetic stance of much of past American theology seemingly has hindered, to some extent, American theological development.

The university must have the strength to follow the presumptions of its own intellectual inquiry. I remember a significant comment by an American theologian that a bishop's role is pastoral rather than academic. The university must use the tools of the scholar. It cannot call on the bishop's authority when it is unable to refute positions and arguments on intellectual grounds.

I see university personnel as part of a community within the wider community of the Church. Perhaps the picture is better painted by describing university men and women as two-world people. One is an arena of free inquiry geared for intellectual development and competence. The other is part of the Church offering service to the community, but with a conscious balance of responsibility. These worlds exist together, hardly in opposition or contradiction, but doubtless in tension. The pattern seems an old one with models from the relationship of magisterium and theologian, of town and gown. I think we are beyond apologizing for this state of affairs and past the expectation that these elements will move to resolution.

II

The major service provided to the Church by the university seems, obviously, the work of teaching. One would expect a university graduate to be a man or woman of faith, cultivated, critical, and mature. Like any Catholic school, however, it is limited in what it can do for religious development. It presupposes a believing student. It is not so well adapted to evangelizing as are some other agencies in the Catholic community.

There is abundant illustration, however, that the university can deepen the commitment of faith.

The material from the National Opinion Research Center of the University of Chicago, *Catholicism, 1963–1974*, by Andrew M. Greeley and William C. McCready demonstrates the liturgical appreciation and social sensitivity of the Catholic college graduate. Deepening of commitment to Church, to parish, to diocese, to religious practice and to family values on the part of Catholic graduates has certainly been within my experience. Catholic college education has effectively developed in many a sense of Christian vocation about work and careers.

The current scene as we all know presents a troubled picture. The Greeley-McCready Report offers statistics that should be of concern to the Catholic institution of higher learning, namely, that the decline in Mass attendance but, more significantly, the departure of membership from the Church takes place in greater numbers among the young and among those who have college educations. Factors involved here are complex and, to their own degree, mysterious. I would suggest, however, to university people an examination of their own relationship to the local Church and particularly the way the university views the local Church. It should be critical, but sympathetic. It should also, to some extent, be involved lest its observations and evaluations be a constant judgment.

I would note, almost in passing, other contributions of the university. Student activities in the 1960's were a particular illustration of highly motivated service in tutoring programs, in working in parish CCD activities, recreational areas, welfare, convalescent care, and contribution to the struggle of the farm workers in California. Along lines somewhat related, the Catholic universities have, perhaps, an unheralded record of reaching out to enable minority students to attend college and to provide from private education's currently restricted means commendable scholarship programs.

I am mindful too in these days in liturgical change and institutional self-evaluation of the innovative liturgical experience that the campus ministry at the Catholic college can often provide. Undoubtedly, this has been with and without local parish approval and both with and without the proper role of the university chapel. It has been on balance, I believe, a benefit.

More to the point is the current contribution of the university through continuing education. This growing work, of course, has not been without its precedents. Our own northern California area had a good experience in the labor schools of the 1930s and 1940s. The local university, for some years, provided for the Newman students on the state college campus in the same city tuition-free night school in theology and Church history.

Continuing education today has a significant place in the training of religious educators, providing courses both in theology, scripture and the methodology of teaching. Additionally, programs reach to adults in other ways to be noted including family life, business, and degrees for adult women.

Special mention should go to the renewal of priestly training. Programs now range from months of intensive education to summer courses, one and two-week workshops, and weekends on a variety of contemporary interests. A university in the West sponsors a traveling faculty to neighboring dioceses offering to clergy and religious the opportunity to earn master's degrees in the teaching of theology and in pastoral counseling.

III

Lastly, I would reflect on the role of the university in the relationship of Church and world.

Social concern is a familiar theme. None of us would be surprised by the remarks to the World Council of Churches in Nairobi by Bishop Mortimer Arias of the Evangelical Methodist Church of Bolivia, who described evangelism as not just announcement and prophetic denouncement or witness or conversion, but "participation in the struggle for a more just and human life inspired by the purpose of God." At risk of superfluity, I would add a quotation from the Synod Document of 1971 on *Justice in the World*,

> The mission of preaching the gospel dictates, at the present time, that we should dedicate ourselves to the liberation of man even in his present existence in the world, for unless the Christian message of love and justice shows its effectiveness through action in the cause of justice in the world, it will only with difficulty gain credibility with the men of our times.

The concept, familiar as it is, needs a good deal of attention by the leadership of the Church at all levels. The Report of Andrew Greeley and William McCready, already alluded to, indicates that 50 percent of our Catholic people are positive about the discussion of social issues in the pulpit, 50 percent negative. Additionally, Avery Dulles in his book *Models of the Church* points to the theological questions that surround the notion of Church as servant, and the weakness of the scriptural background for this particular model. Our problems remain both in thought and in practice with this concept.

The bishops have given evidence of attempting to incorporate the theology of the Servant Church in their pastoral practice. The bicentennial celebration with its theme of "Liberty and Justice for All" is

139

aiming its program to parishes, to six regional hearings that have recently been completed, and to a national meeting in October of 1976 to plan pastoral guidelines for the five years to follow. In addition, bishops' statements in recent years on unemployment, housing, abortion, and world hunger are among some indications of direction being taken.

The awareness of university personnel is similar. The November 1972 statement of the International Federation of Catholic Universities, speaking of the institutions' academic role, says that

> If a university wishes to fulfill its vocation to be an effective instrument of human progress and to not remain on the fringe of the dynamic force of history, it must direct its research and especially interdisciplinary research toward the urgent problems of social development.

The university in that same statement has its own awareness of its particular qualification to offer "provisions of expert consultation to the Church and its responsibility to make its scholarly discoveries available to the decision makers in Church and Society." From the point of view of the Catholic community the university seems such an obvious resource. It should serve as collaborator and sharer of responsibility. Furthermore, the university can offer its contribution not just in the area of research. I realize the importance of that, but I also feel that the ordinary competence and wisdom of the teaching staff in theology, law, sociology, economics, political science, and medicine offer rich potential in developing our consciousness of the social role of the Church and the practical implementation of that responsibility.

As I review the university's potential, I recollect the prudent observation of the English Dominican, Father Vincent McNabb, "The primary thing is not to tell everyone his duty, but to do one's own."

I would, therefore, acknowledge the responsibility of the bishops at the national level to investigate needed areas of research on major concerns perhaps after the fashion of the breadth of study done on the American priesthood.

Operations exist in the American Church that can be instruments of collaboration between university and Church. At the national level there is the United States Catholic Conference, an organizational structure to serve "the public, educational, and social concerns of the Church at national and regional levels and, as appropriate, at diocesan levels."

The Conference operates with staff and committees in the areas of justice and peace, social development, and wide ranging bank of interests.

The local Church has engendered a variety of tools as well, including diocesan and parish committees for social justice and departments of pastoral planning. Where these groups are alive, action and judgment take place in a wide area. University competence could offer a testing of decisions. The Apostolic Delegate at the November Bishops' meeting encouraged intellectual underpinning for a response to practical and urgent social problems. He warned against speaking on topics without prior study.

At the state level, there now exist 31 Catholic Conferences. Most of these have sprung up in the last decade. They vary in size and structure, but all are concerned with relating the Church to legislatures and to state departments and agencies. They serve additionally to inform the Catholic people on issues and to assist the bishops in evaluating and offering direction on matters of major concern.

These structures offer potential collaboration. At the same time, one would have to acknowledge the cooperation already existing between State Conferences and seminaries, law faculties, and a variety of individuals in the academic world. In our own state the Conference and one Catholic university have begun explorations in areas of mutual benefit.

The mention of these latter instruments brings up a point that I feel should be delineated and emphasized. This is the question that arises, in conjunction with the work of these agencies, of the role of the Church in politics. To move into social responsibility seems to me to accept political involvement. The Church's role demands that it be in the pluralistic dialogue at effective points. At times, its responsibility will be other than statement or evaluation and will move to action.

On the political question all of us express reserve. The Synod of 1971 speaks of clergy needing generally to distance themselves from the political scene. The document from the International Federation of Catholic Universities describes research directed to social development, "not so much in finding political solutions to problems as in laying the scientific foundations for their solutions."

This distance is comfortable and neatly precise. It is not, however, accurate. Although the Church is adverse to supporting candidates and parties and is reluctant, generally, to enter legislative questions, it is active in particulars. It hid its role very little in the issue of tax credit for parents of nonpublic school students. Both the United States Catholic

Conference and the State Conferences are vocal on the matter of illegal aliens and the current bill, H.R. 8713. The California Bishops participated in the passage of the Agricultural Labor Relations Act of 1975. The Pro Life Program of the bishops, nationally, is widely interpreted as clear entry into the political area.

Furthermore, the Catholic community, in good part, expects leadership to act. This past year there were two bills in California of particular interest that were neither opposed nor supported by the bishops. One dealt with the repeal of the law against private sexual conduct. The other allowed physicians to distribute contraceptives to minors without parents' consent, in a state whose Supreme Court had earlier declared legitimacy of minors procuring abortions without parental knowledge. Reaction of parents and others in the community, especially those critical of the Conference's neutral position, manifested their clear judgment on the responsibility of Church leadership.

Political questions that are our common burden whether we are university or ecclesiastical people deal with a variety of issues. Among the foremost are those in the medical-moral field. We deal here not merely with the moral issues involved, but what is the proper expression of these values in law. There are matters of women's rights and the ERA, tax reform, needs of the aged, changes in criminal justice. There are issues relatively untouched by Catholic presence such as nuclear power and general matters of ecology.

There are more than merely practical questions involved. Together, it seems, we must search for the principles underlying the proper Church role. All of us are comfortable with the notion of the Church and the university developing in the individual a sense of vocational responsibility. We are, however, now at the point of asking what is the responsibility of Church as Church. This raises questions of what right does the Church have in dialogue. It makes us ask what is the responsibility of the Church in legislative hearings or in the halls of law makers. We have to ask whether the Church should remain in the realm of discussion and argument or whether it can legitimately use political force. We face all these questions furthermore in the real realm of tax exemptions. Here we ask what risks are proper, what rights do we have to exemptions, what limitations are tolerable under the matter of exemptions, what freedoms are threatened without such exemptions.

Universities and chanceries, no doubt, have a varied history of relationships. There have been times of cooperation, of civility, of indifference, of mutual tolerance that may have moved to the edge of proper Christian practice. The detachment of the university from the local Church can be one question. I would concede, on the other hand, the comment of Father Ladislas Orsy about the little urgency felt in the Church to make itself ''university minded.'' I feel, and it is my desire to feel, that a period of improved collaboration lies ahead of us.

Catholicism: Its Place in the Contemporary University

Donald P. Merrifield, S.J.

The time has come to confront and overcome our defensiveness about being Catholic universities and our anxieties about the survival of our institutions. Plagued as we have been for too many years with upheavals in the university world and in the Catholic Church, forever seeking to define for ourselves exactly what is required to make us Catholic in terms of required courses, university policies, or public declarations, financially threatened, we need most of all to become aware of unique power that Catholicism can give to an educational enterprise. We need to find ways to develop that power within our institutions. Without this uniqueness, this added dimension which touches all of the university, our Catholic institutions of higher education have no reason to exist. Some may linger on as members of that group of formerly religiously-sponsored institutions, but such independent colleges and universities themselves stand a good chance to be taken over by state systems or squeezed out of existence in the years ahead, except for some truly outstanding institutions.

I am not asserting that a rediscovery of the significance of Catholicism for our academic enterprise will save our institutions, but that, without such a rediscovery, there is no firm reason to expect that we will continue to exist. I assert that the passing of the Catholic colleges and universities would be a very sad thing, not just for the Catholic world, but for the academic world itself. For, and this is my thesis, Catholic institutions can and should do a very unique thing in higher education, a thing which no other institution is capable of doing and a thing which is very worth doing.

My conviction that Catholicism brings a unique and extremely valuable element into the academic world is rooted in the importance of the ultimate questions aroung which all religious traditions are formed, and which I find most sharply posed in my own tradition, as well as in what may be called Catholicism's worldliness. By the worldliness of Catholicism, I mean the full variety of interactions between Catholic belief and tradition and the world in which it has lived and grown. Always affirming the transcendent quality of the gospel about which this tradition is centered, Catholicism, not without long hesitation and questioning at many periods of its history, has also affirmed and made its own the best of human thought and creativity throughout history. Without losing touch with the ultimate realities which are of its essence, without reducing the mystery of God to a human phenomenon or to some vague mysteriousness within the universe, without limiting man to a passing event on an undistinguished planet of a minor star, Catholicism has, with at times extreme caution, met each emerging facet of human history and culture, carefully separated the wheat from the chaff, the humanly good from the destructive, and integrated these human and worldly elements into its own understanding of human life and destiny, its modes of expression and its wisdom.

One of the greatest achievements of Catholicism in its history—even from a purely secular viewpoint—was the origin and development of the university five hundred years before the Reformation began. No other religious tradition—Hinduism, Buddhism, Islam, Confucianism—took the mind of man, the *human* world so seriously. Why? Because Catholic Christianity had affirmed that God had become fully man in Jesus Christ and struggled through many centuries to defend that humanness and the essential goodness of all creation.

Within the present world of academe there is no other religious tradition with such an intellectual character, with such a universality, with such an openness, at least in the long view, to all things human as the Catholic tradition. The colleges and universities sponsored by the more fundamentalist churches may be less worldly than Catholic institutions, more straightforward in their statements and their policies as Christian institutions, but, it seems to me they lack the ability to bridge the gap between the secular and the profane, between divine and human initiative. This lack, I believe, is rooted in their theological differences with Catholics. I might go so far as to place the essential difference in our teachings on the effects of original sin on the human intellect and will and on the redemptive activity of the Spirit of God outside of the Christian community.

Unfortunately, however, I believe most American Catholics do not know the richness of their tradition and have become rather parochial in their own experience of Catholicism. This is quite understandable, if lamentable, given our insular and defensive posture in this country, the overly legalistic sense of the faith with which most of us were brought up, and the lack of an historical or international view of Catholicism. I would like to think that the opportunity was never greater, however, for us in the Catholic colleges and universities to rise above our parochial limitations and rediscover the power that this tradition in its full range and variety, its affirmation of the human and the more than human, can bring to the life of our institutions.

In fact, the vitality of the Catholic centers of higher education is crucial to American Catholicism's coming of age. If these institutions can combine an understanding of the Catholic tradition with serious reflection upon and responsible criticism of contemporary thought, values, and culture, they will not only do a great service to the Catholic community, but also be of unique service to the entire academic world and to our society.

It is sad that Catholics have been so easily caught up in "trendiness," in an over-eager attempt to be contemporary, in an embarrassment before a secular world about the other-worldliness and moral positions of our tradition, in a false ecumenism which reduces all the rich subtlety of Catholicism to a genial sense of brotherhood. Of course, we have suffered severe shocks to our certainties in recent years, severe loss of self-confidence, but I believe our reactions have been at least in part due to our limited and parochial Catholicism. If we had had some larger view and experience of Catholicism, a dynamic image of the Church with a sense of its profound humanness and vitality, we Catholics might not have been in such a constant state of turmoil and self-searching as we have been in recent years.

In the contemporary university world, we most often find the reemphasis on values and on moral education coming from outside the Catholic institutions, whose members run after this development rather than serve in its front ranks. Similarly, we may come across a reaffirmation of metaphysics and ethics as central to education in such a book as E.F. Schumacher's *Small is Beautiful* long after we have allowed these key human disciplines to become lifeless or fall completely out of our curricula. Even in religious studies, where we have been tempted to provide a dispassionate, anthropocentric approach to religious phenomena or to reduce our rich theological tradition to biblical and religious experience courses, we in Catholic higher education may find ourselves being awakened to what we have already lost or are presently losing from the movements taking place in the nonreligious institutions. True, we have gone through intellectual, social, and religious crises. True, we cannot just teach the old courses in the old way. True, all of us suffer from uncertainties. All this is the very reason that the time is ripe for a revival of intellectualism, of critical thinking, of clarification of values and commitments, a revival which, according to my thesis, can and should take place most powerfully at those centers in which the ultimate questions of God, salvation, sin, good and evil, and human freedom and dignity still stand to confront and challenge us. These questions are not being ignored by Russian intellectuals such as those whose essays appear in the recent book, *From Under the Rubble*, edited by Solzhenitzen. If we at American Catholic institutions treat these questions as curious, peripheral, irrelevant, or meaningless, then we truly ought to cease to exist.

How intellectual reflection which is integrative and which is open to the fullness of human experience and keeps central the ultimate questions should be carried out at each campus is difficult to predetermine. But it should characterize the Catholic university. Some institutions should have research centers, some will make use of interdisciplinary courses, some others special days of serious total university attention to key issues in all their dimensions. Certainly, faculty do not communicate with one another enough at most institutions, sharing the insights and methodology of their disciplines. Much less are they liable to share their deepest personal convictions and their doubts.

The university should be a learning community, a discovering community. It is not a church, nor a business enterprise, nor a little kingdom of its own. In a university, Catholicism cannot be understood as attempting to accomplish what it does in the monastery or the diocese or the parish church. It is not enough that there be pastoral care and some Christian community and preaching of the gospel on the campus. Neither, on the other hand, should a forced and fearful traditionalism masquerading as orthodoxy be the characteristic of the Catholic institution, assured by a type of control foreign to the academic environment. There should be careful presentation of the authentic teaching of the Catholic Church. Academic responsibility demands such care in all teaching, with clear distinctions between what is established and authentic and what is opinion and speculation. This much should be the hallmark of any good university.

What the Catholic university should foster, beyond the pastoral care of those who wish it and beyond careful presentation of Catholic—and all other—thinking and teaching, is the integration of human and divine, of the immediate and the ultimate, of faith and reason. For humanity cannot be fully understood or appreciated except in a religious context and the religious questions are finally the important ones.

But universities cannot be just isolated "think tanks," even if the thinking includes ultimate questions. They are also producers of men and women who will be active in the professions within our society. They must also be centers of responsible and careful criticism upon all aspects of society. This is especially true of the religiously-oriented university. Our graduates, if they have experienced a fully human education, should be change agents within our society for a more just and human world. The present concern about teaching professional ethics should extend to moral education in general, touching upon all aspects of social responsibility.

At the present time, when our students seem to be apathetic, if not totally indifferent or cynical, with respect to social and political issues, and, according to one newspaper account, seeking "only a job, a home in the suburbs, and not to be hassled," it may be difficult to work up an enthusiasm about social criticism and social and moral education as a function of colleges and universities. But, a Catholic institution of higher education would be especially failing if it did not act as a critic of man's political, social, technological, and cultural enterprises and teach its students this ability to question and judge, joined with a commitment to take effective action against the destructive and the oppressive and the inhuman. We cannot ignore Catholicism's strong stand against many aspects and values of the contemporary and self-satisfied society of which we are a part and claim to be authentic as a Catholic university. If our education does not make any impact on the values of our graduates, especially social values, we should indeed go out of business. If our only function has been to bring immigrant peoples into mainstream, middle-class America with a certain religiosity such as is still appropriate and respectable, we may indeed have succeeded. But has it been worth it? I, for one, hope we have done more and know that we must do more in the future, if we are to survive.

With the almost overwhelming emphasis I have put upon the Catholicism of our universities and colleges, where does that leave those who are not Catholic in our student bodies, on our faculty and staffs, among our trustees and benefactors? Our fellow Christians and those of other faiths or indeed of no religious faith can and should make very important contributions to our educational institutions. They bring us a healthy diversity of points of view, keep us from being isolated and turned in upon ourselves, and, at the same time, often challenge us to be true to the best in our tradition, to be authentically Catholic. Although it would be impossible to have a vital center of Catholic intellectual reflection and social criticism without a significant number of articulate and committed Catholics, I suspect that such a center could not be vital, also, without the active involvement of those who are not Catholic. However, all those who become part of a Catholic university or college should be aware of particular character that Catholicism gives—or should give—to the institution and its concerns, as we Catholics should be aware of the value of the ecumenical character they give to our common academic venture. If it is important to make it clear that we are not the sort of religious college in which all are required to go to chapel and in which no dangerous thought can be broached, it is even more important to make it clear to all who become involved with us that we are not just a secular school with a dash of churchiness on the side or for special occasions.

Actions, as always, speak louder than words and if, as a matter of fact, we are not at all the sort of thing a Catholic university should and can be, but rather a very parochial and protective little oasis with lots of Catholic activities and externals, but little serious interaction between our religiosity and our academic ventures, no proclamations will make us other than what we actually have become. If we are a second-rate or even first-rate secular school, with a few signs of our Catholic heritage left, again our self-definition will have a very hollow ring about it.

Let the Catholic university, then, be faithful to the fullness of its Catholicism and to the power of that tradition to affirm the goodness of human culture, while redeeming it from its limitations. Let such a university not be parochial, in the sense of narrowly sectarian, timid, afraid to face difficult questions. Let it be intellectually honest and academically responsible, searching for the truth in all areas of human experience, insofar as we may discover it, confronting moral issues and reflecting upon all in the light of religious insights and values. In short, then, let the Catholic university be truly catholic, open to all who want to be part of it and concerned about everything human, not in a spirit of mere intellectual curiosity, but in a true love for man and his works and his struggles, for each man and woman in his or her longing for justice, true freedom and an understanding of the full dignity and destiny of each and all.

The Catholic People and the Catholic University

Michael Novak

I

No part of the American population is more important to the American future than that part—a full quarter, or even one-third—whose culture is Catholic. Reasons for this judgment may be argued elsewhere. Suffice it to say that Catholics are centrally located, relatively concentrated, highly active politically, and more than Protestants or Jews "independent" in political affiliation—a truly impressive swing force in politics. And also in culture. As Catholics tip in the next two decades, so will the nation.

The Catholic university, meanwhile, has for some two decades concentrated rather more on "entering the mainstream" of American life than on articulating the distinctively Catholic cultures of the Catholic peoples. These varied cultures are, e.g., Hispanic, Eastern European, Italian, Celtic, Germanic, French, British, Black, etc. (in roughly that order, assigned by relative proportion of Catholics). This recent emphasis was not only useful. It was indispensable. Only so could Catholic institutions raise themselves to culturally respectable and seriously taken standards. No one doubts that at least the major Catholic universities of the land now rank among the best of the state universities, and that the Catholic colleges are at least as good as, often better than, their neighbors. Catholic institutions are on everybody's intellectual map, in every region of the nation.

Still, there is dissatisfaction. We await a new direction. "Entering the mainstream" isn't good enough. "Being taken seriously" is good. But now that we have the public's attention, so to speak, what ought we to do?

II

On the part of the American bishops, it might be presumptuous to speak. Still, an outsider's point of view, however off the mark, might be useful, at least as a means of clarifying the true picture by rejecting a false one.

Since the Vatican Council, now descended ten years into history, the American Catholic bishops have faced at least three unprecedented cultural problems. First, public attention and, indeed, much good will, have been lavished upon things Catholic. Compared to the situation of, say, 1958 (the date of the Fund for the Republic's consultation on Catholicism), things Catholic are vastly better reported, understood, and sympathetically received by the American public, both ordinary and elite. A vigorous anti-Catholicism still exists, especially among elites, but it would have been naive to have expected it to dissolve in ten short years. Besides, there are good *reasons* for others in America to be a little wary of the Catholic people. Group conflict and shifting group coalitions are vital parts of the American system. The American bishops, in any case, have been in the national spotlight as never before. Favorably or unfavorably, their actions are reported as news.

Secondly, administrative problems of a new type have multiplied. The turmoil implicit in the new forms of collegiality; in the new ''contract'' with the modern age that led so many of the clergy, religious, and laity to question whether and how they were still Catholic or wished to keep to their earlier vows; and in the new liturgy, etc., would have been enough to present administrative problems of the greatest magnitude. In addition, the changing economic order (making costs of every sort soar) and the vast exurban migration have drastically compounded the problems of finances; e.g., in the opening of new buildings, and the closing of old.

Thirdly, the rapid diffusion of cultural symbols and ideas through higher education, class mobility, and the new media has dramatically altered the relation of preachers to their people. Ideas and perceptions of great spiritual moment, for good or ill, reach the people directly, in every institutional interstice of their lives: at work, in school, at play, in their homes. In older times, one could censure books, censure attendance at films, and in other ways somewhat control the flow of percept, feeling, image, and idea to enter the lives of people. No more. The role of a bishop can scarcely be, in practice, a ''protective'' role. In the new situation, a certain combativeness, aggressiveness, and competitiveness are required of those who wish to be heard—reasonableness, accuracy, adroitness, and a command of what is atrociously called "public relations." The air is filled with messages. In a relatively free market, one must compete to be heard, to be respected, and to be taken to heart.

How to solve any one of these problems would tax persons of genius. How to address all three of them at once is beyond the strength of all. Not that efforts are not being made, efforts that in any case are relatively effective. (The public ranks "organized religion," in an age of high anti-institutional animus, as the institution for which it has more respect than any other). But we do not have to flatter one another. The task is not being met with anything like the effectiveness required. The potential decline of Catholic life is all too vivid—a financial decline, a decline in churchgoing, a decline in vocations, a decline in knowledge of and deep resonance with the best traditions of our people, a decline in political and social potency, a decline in public estimation, a decline in exemplary Catholic living.

In my mind's eye, the bishops are like a man with only ten fingers trying to cover a sieve with thirty holes that need attention.

III

It is in this context that I imagine the universities and the bishops turning to each other. (Incidentally, I include the state and private secular universities. Catholics pay at least a quarter of all tax monies. There are many areas of research, intellectual tradition, and investigation in which the secular universities do, with respect to Catholic matters, a less than adequate job. The Catholic peoples and their traditions are relatively unstudied, relatively neglected. The bishops and the people have a right to request a greater output from institutions supported by the public—more accurate empirical research concerning the Catholic population, more full and accurate treatment of Catholic cultures and traditions in the curricula and in higher studies. On another level, personnel, a double standard is at present quite effective: The relative absence of women or blacks is taken as a prima facie sign of discrimination; but the even more marked absence of Catholics is taken as a prima facie case of Catholic inadequacy. Catholics could be, and ought to be, far more insistent that tax monies in education, public broadcasting, the foundations, and elsewhere be used equitably, and in due proportion represent the Catholic quarter of the population in benefits accrued.)

What can the bishops offer the Catholic colleges and universities? Most of all, a warm invitation to come and be of assistance. To set up seminars in nearby parishes. To provide lecture series, study groups, and research enterprises. To develop economic, social, and cultural plans for the future of the Catholic people and their institutions. To develop political cadre to become sophisticated about contemporary political issues, techniques, and organizations. Compared to the Quakers, the upper-class Protestants of the Northeast (so much supported by the investigations of the Foundations), the Jews, and others, the Catholic people are not politically or organizationally sophisticated. The trained personnel of the universities could help to make the Catholic people a more enlightened, sophisticated, and democratic body, to the greater benefit of the nation. For the nation depends on an enlightened citizenry committed to democratic methods and skillful in their employment.

It is necessary to underscore this point. More than many realize, the latent purpose and the actual effect of most education in the U.S. is to make "Uncle Tommaso's" and "Aunt Cecilia's" of our population—to educate them *away from* their families, neighborhoods, and traditions. This process is improperly called "secularization." It has a basis in class realities. The best and the brightest are skimmed off the top, handsomely rewarded, and led to serve, not their own people, but the interests of the fast-living, prosperous, professional classes of the nation. Education is the screening device for siphoning off potential leaders of the people (in the "subcultures" of America) and binding them to the "superculture." The problem is not so much that such successful leaders become "secularized," for many of them do not, but rather that their primary public loyalties are bound to interests not those of the families and the peoples from whom they derive. They may be personally pious, privately religious, and even generous in the donation of time, energy, and money to their alma mater; but the true effect of their professional work often works contrary to the interests of ordinary people. The professional classes of the U.S., for all their good qualities (we have much to be grateful for in our elites), are injuriously detached from the perspectives, needs, and interests of those they have left behind.

In this sense, the bishops should not underestimate the importance of giving assignments to, and making requests of, professionals in the Catholic university. Many are eager to be of service to the people. Few other institutions in our society allow them, or encourage them, to be so. The bishops have a right, duty even, to nourish a sense of service to their own people (and through them to all peoples) among Catholic professionals and students in formation. The leadership of the bishops is essential. Mainly, they must *ask* and, perhaps, outline some initial projects: requesting help in gathering specific information, designing specific plans, etc. Once the process has been started, many fresh minds will come up with other ideas of what can be done.

IV

What can the universities offer to the bishops? I would propose a long ten-year effort to strengthen the cultural life of the entire Catholic people in the nation (and, of course, other Americans with them). Who are we? What has our history been? What are our needs? Which among several directions ought we to take? Much is to be gained by observing the ancient maxim: "Charity begins at home." By concentrating on the Catholic people as a specific case, Catholic universities would: (a) have a distinctive task and make a distinctive contribution; (b) widen the present range of intellectual life and public insight in the nation; (c) have a project large enough to encompass the most generous perspectives, but limited enough to allow for some measures of relative success or failure; (d) be of true service to the Catholic peoples, whom it would be naive to expect others to serve as well; and (e) strengthen a major part of the American population—the part nearest to their own hearts, sensibilities, insights, and responsibilities.

Let me mention just a few of the areas in which creative work might be accomplished in a decade-long concerted project.

1. *Demography*. It is astonishing how poor our information is on the base numbers. Are there 10 million Italian-Americans, or 20? How *many* people have changed their names? How many Americans are Catholic in culture of origin (and still so, unconsciously), even if not practicing these last two generations or so? Is it true that more blacks ages 18–24 are now in college than Slavic or Italian-Americans? Etc.

2. *Opinion and conviction surveys*. A sample of, say, 30,000 Americans could be well-designed so as to cover in significant ways every major religious, cultural, class, regional, income, and educational differentiation, and give us far more accurate tools than we have at present to capture substantial variations in public views—both the transient factors of "opinion" and the more stable factors of "conviction." For example, attitudes on abortion are far more complex and profound than

present surveys allow us to uncover. Similarly, quite false pictures of the Catholic working class are common among elite Americans, and more intelligently designed research might make the accurate picture indisputable.

3. *Urban planning*. Millions of dollars worth of Church investments in inner city land and real estate have been lost through failures to anticipate—and to control—vast urban change since World War II. We may anticipate next the rapid deterioration of the suburban housing stock, often cheaply built and not designed to last. What migrations ought the Church now to begin to prepare for, financially and every other way?

4. *Literature, cinema, and the arts*. The experience of immigration and acculturation among diverse groups of American Catholics has hardly yet been set to paper or captured in film. A people without a literature is a people without a mirror. Works of art heighten our self-knowledge (often by exaggeration or by negative images, to be sure, but indispensably). The dearth of Catholic writers and artists can be overcome with fair rapidity, if audiences demand new works. The explosion of black literature in recent years indicates how much can be done swiftly. Slavic, Hispanic, French, German, and other Catholic cultures need literary and artistic stimulation.

5. *The teaching of religion in public schools, in Catholic schools, in the media, and elsewhere* must take account of all the new stimuli our people encounter. We are not working in a vacuum of messages.

6. *History*. The history of northern urban centers has been written mainly by the classic adversaries of Catholic political movements. "They" are always the good guys, for Reform, morality, decency, and enlightened ways; "we" are always unenlightened. Histories of populism seldom show sophistication about Catholic urban populism. That Catholics are politically more progressive than Protestants, on virtually every index, is plain in voting patterns and in survey research; but intellectual stereotypes of "hard hat," "proto-fascist," "conservative," "hawkish," "backlash," "bluecollar" citizens survive. The socio-political history of the Catholic people has yet to be written. It would tell us a great deal about our strengths and weaknesses.

These suggestions barely scratch the surface. More precise areas of research and planning might easily be elicited.

The important point is to envisage the entire American Catholic intellectual world attempting, over a period of ten years, a sustained cultural, organizational, and intellectual advance of measurable consequence. The aim would be to place ourselves in 1986 at a far more highly developed cultural, intellectual, and political position than in 1976. The leading conception would be: "From the Catholic Quarter: As Americans and as Catholics, we fashion the most intellectually sound and politically creative contribution we can imagine, and place it at the service of our fellow citizens." The bishops would invite, stimulate, and encourage all the Catholic colleges and universities, and their state and private counterparts, to join in these intellectual and organizational efforts. Students, faculties, administrators, publicists would do all they can to study, nourish, organize, assist, and unify the Catholic peoples, transforming their inchoate longings and restless energies into a vital organism of Christian and democratic life.

The project would be conceived as a return for all we have received from America, a gift to America, our contribution. Our active, intelligent, and creative exercise of democratic citizenship—and the deeds and works that flow therefrom—would be the sort of gift this nation was established to elicit. "The land of opportunity was founded so that we might seize its opportunities, not squander them." Opportunity is one thing; use of it another. It would be wrong for us to bury out talents. It may be time to use them to the full.

If every group in America did the same, the nation would be alive and alert and creative, as seldom before in its entire past.

Research in the Church
Most Rev. James S. Rausch

This paper is, in most part, a re-presentation of a talk I delivered at the Catholic University of America on May 13, 1975. The subject of the gathering was interdisciplinary and interuniversity research. The occasion was an important one where leaders of Catholic universities in this country discussed common concerns regarding research.

In my perception of things there is today, as in the past, a clear desire on the part of the university community to play an active and creative role in the life of the Christian community. Through the vision of Vatican II a concerted effort was made to restate the identity of the Catholic university, culminating in the 1972 statement entitled, "The Catholic University in the Modern World."[1] Since that time, attention has been devoted to rendering that identity correct. The present meeting on research is a significant stage in this process.

In view of this, it may prove helpful to look back for a moment into the long experience of our predecessors in the faith, to draw from them some insight concerning the crucial role of men's intellectual effort in God's loving providence. This should help in appreciating more fully the role of research in the Church, as well as the contribution which this meeting might make to its growth.

THE HERITAGE

The Fathers: The Role of Intellectual Development in the Life of Faith

John Courtney Murray, in his Yale lectures on *The Problem of God, Yesterday and Today*,[2] described masterfully the crucial juncture at

[1] *NCEA, College Newsletter* XXX (n. 3, 1973), 1–10.
[2] (New Haven: Yale University Press, 1969).

which the Church made its irrevocable decision concerning the role of intellectual development in the life of faith. Fittingly, the decision was made in the Church's highest forum, at the Council of Nicaea, and in treating the greatest mystery, the Trinity. The situation was as follows. In the scriptures and the expression of the early Church, Christ had been referred to in relational and descriptive terms: he is Emmanuel—or, God-with-us—he is Savior and he is Lord. It was the strongly stated position of Eusebius of Caesarea and his followers that nothing more than these biblical terms should be used.

Nonetheless, implicit in this description of Christ-in-relation-to-us was a definition of Christ-in-himself and of the relation of the Son to the Father. Inevitably, once the logic of the issue and the dynamism of the human mind made explicit this ontological question, it had to be answered. What is more, it had to be answered in faith, for anything less would negate the life of faith from within. If Christ as Son is not God but man only, then we are not redeemed and our faith is in vain.

The Second and Third Century attempts to answer this question had been inadequate either because, as with Tertullian, they remained subject to the inherent limitations of biological and anthropomorphic metaphors or because, as with Origen, they simply adopted the Middle Platonist notion of emanation with its implication that the Son could be only a diminished likeness of the Father, a God of the second order. For his part, Arius did not hesitate to speak of Christ as the "perfect creature" who, at one time, was not.

In these circumstances it was clear to the Council Fathers at Nicaea that the understanding of the faith had to grow so that its sense would remain unchanged. Because they considered no longer adequate the expression "like (*homoies*) the Father" they took the decisive step of adding to the Creed the ontological term, "consubstantial (*homoousion*) with the Father."[3] In so doing they recognized that the answer in faith (as Courtney Murray puts it) "had to be given, not in the empirical categories of experience, the relational category of presence, or even, the dynamic categories of power and function but in the ontological category of substance, which is a category of being."[4]

Effectively, the Church had crossed the Rubicon. It would not, because it could not, be outside the development of the human intellect. On the contrary, the development of the capacity of the human mind to

[3]H. Denziger, *Enchiridion Symbolorum* (Rome: Herder, 1958).
[4]Murray, p. 45.

analyze and to question was recognized as integral to the progressive articulation of the meaning of the faith. In Courtney Murray's language, "By sanctioning the status of the ontological mentality in the field of faith, Nicaea also established the statute of the philosophical reason in the field of theology,"[5] from Augustine's use of Platonism, through Thomas' use of Aristotelianism to Rahner's use of phenomenology.[6] In a word, it made theology in the strict sense possible. What is more, it implied a charter for the role of the many specialized bodies of knowledge (e.g., the sciences, which would be developed in the future) and for the research work carried out in each.

The Church in America: The Universities

We, in this country, are heirs and pasticipants in this rich tradition. In the last century and in the midst of a vast flood of Catholic immigrants the importance which the Church attached to intellectual growth was reflected in the founding and rapid expansion of the Catholic educational system. It was wisely appreciated then that a truly Christian understanding could not consist in a certain "amount" of religion externally juxtaposed to a developed pattern of secular disciplines. On the contrary, the growth in Christian awareness by the Church in this country was seen to require that theology, at its highest level of scholarship and research, be in contact with philosophy and vice versa. It was understood further that these two disciplines could not be carried for-

---

[5]*Ibid.*, p. 52.

[6]I do not consider the project of Saint Augustine in his *City of God* to be other than an extended statement of the meaning of the terms "Pantokrator" used in the early Credo and of "Monarchy" used by Dionysius of Rome in the middle of the third century. They expressed the power of the one supreme Lord as generously creative and provident whose active power rules all things, physical and human; Augustine was able to articulate this more amply by means of the understanding developed in the philosophies available by his time. With their help he was able to develop at length the meaning of the faith for the development of human society in history with its inherent struggle faithfully to realize its life in the image of God.

Nor are the great works of Thomas and Scotus other than further elaborations which become possible as responses to the more detailed and coordinated questioning which the introduction of Aristotelian thought made possible. They were saints and doctors in no divided or separated sense; theirs was a learned holiness. It is precisely as such that they have provided the light which has aided many to understand better the meaning of their life in God.

ward without a close reciprocal relationship with research in the arts and in the physical, psychological, and social sciences.

Newman reminded us, more than a century ago, of the interdependence of knowledge and the necessity of unifying the various areas of human learning. He wrote:

> The assemblage of sciences. . . may be said to be *in equilibrio*, as long as all its portions are secured to it. Take away one of them, and that one so important in the catalogue as Theology, and disorder and ruin at once ensue. There is no middle state between an *equilibrium* and chaotic confusion; one science is ever pressing upon another, unless kept in check; and the only guarantee of truth is the cultivation of them all. And such is the office of a University.[7]

He spoke specifically of the relationship of the intellectual and religious spheres in a sermon preached in the spring of 1856:

> I want to destroy that diversity of centres, which puts everything into confusion by creating a contrariety of influences. I wish the same spots and the same individuals to be at once oracles of philosophy and shrines of devotion. It will not satisfy me, what satisfies so many, to have two independent systems, intellectual and religious, going at once side by side, by a sort of division of labour, and only accidentally brought together. . . . I want the same roof to contain both the intellectual and moral discipline. Devotion is not a sort of finish given to the sciences; nor is science a sort of feather in the cap, if I may so express myself, an ornament and set-off to devotion. I want the intellectual layman to be religious, and the devout ecclesiastic to be intellectual.[8]

In a word, reflection on revelation, in order to be adequate at any time, requires the full panoply of methods developed thus far by the human mind for investigating the single areas of reality. Indeed, the foundation of the national Catholic University eighty-five years ago, with its pattern of graduate departments in all areas of the arts and

[7]Newman, *Discourses on University Education*.
[8]Newman, *Sermons Preached on Various Occasions*.

sciences, is testimony that this has been the fundamental conviction of the Church in the United States. It is a conviction that has been reexpressed continually in the early founding and impressive growth of other such institutions spanning the country from Washington to Washington, and of which you are the representatives.

What is more, this development could not have taken place without the active, dedicated, and self-sacrificing support of the total Church in our country. The parish collections, the door-to-door drives, the extensive sacrifices by parents, the dedicated lives of the many lay and religious faculty members, and the benefactions, taken together, proclaim one abiding *sensus fidelium,* namely, that Catholic universities are essential for providing the understanding we need of the meaning of our Christian life today.

In this connection, the Catholic universities (as well as other Catholic intellectual institutes), have a right to receive from the official Church, and indeed all parts of it, both recognition and support for their singular role. This, unfortunately, has not always been forthcoming. A friendly and judicious observer of the American scene has reminded us of truths that should not be forgotten except at our peril. Archbishop Jean Jadot, addressing the November 1975 meeting of the Catholic Bishops of the United States, spoke as follows:

> In our technological society, with its ever growing desire for a life without discomfort or sacrifice, the old danger of anti-intellectualism is always rampant. Perhaps, what is even worse, we are exposed to a pseudo-intellectualism which encourages us to speak out on almost any topic without prior, in-depth study. Too often, the discipline required for serious study is lacking.
>
> Moreover, the need for action on the urgent social problems of our day could lead to a neglect of scholarly interest and research. I am convinced that the Church must be active in the struggle against injustice and poverty and in the defense of human rights, especially the right to life. But, I am equally convinced that we must encourage intellectual inquiry and strongly support Catholic institutions engaged in scientific studies.

We in this room, above all, must never forget the deep dependence that exists between the urgency of this need for research and the provision of the facilities with which we work. Indeed, this very urgency requires that we assess the situation. Certainly, much has been done. By the turn of the century, one of three psychological laboratories in the United States was in operation at a Catholic university. The writing of the original *Catholic Encyclopedia* was a prodigious mobilization of Catholic scholarship throughout the world. Today, however, given the quandaries in the Church, the nation and the world, we must ask—as do those in other universities—if we have kept up with the problems generated by our new capabilities: are we doing enough and are we doing it well enough; are we directing our capabilities to the real needs and are we doing so in a manner that is creative or destructive? We need to think about that at this meeting.

In "taking stock" note must be made of the elements of diffidence and possibly even of suspicion which, at times, have been manifest between those doing research and all other levels of the Church. The excellent papers prepared by Drs. Bonneau and Ladrière for the colloquy at Grottaferrata, in identifying some of the bases for this phenomenon, call to mind ways of overcoming it which, I believe, can be developed in some of the remaining sections of this talk.

At this point, I will simply identify a few factors which generate this diffidence. On the one hand, it is important that in the work of the researcher, the realm of the imagination have full play. He must be free to formulate hypotheses and to test them according to the norms of truth appropriate to the specific discipline. This has led those in research, rightly, to guard their freedom jealously. Without it, their work becomes impossible. On the other hand, it is necessary that researchers qualify the results of their work as hypothetical. This has not always been done with clarity, if at all; moreover, it must be remembered that the meaning of such a qualification is difficult to appreciate for those who have not themselves developed habits of research. Secondly, the researcher does not share with the bishops the immediacy of their pastoral role. As a result, it is often difficult for the researcher to understand the bishops' intense concern regarding the effects of scholars' work upon those poorly prepared to interpret its implications.

In this combination of differentiated capabilities and concern lie the seeds for misunderstanding and distrust which have disturbed what rightfully should be a fully positive relationship. Indeed, it may have involved universities, both Catholic and secular, in the worldwide alienation from the general population, in the late sixties, and dissuaded some members of the Church from looking to the universities for the help they need. The resolution of this problem, as with all redemptive acts, must begin with a recognition of the roots of the problem and an acknowledgment of past failings. I sense a readiness to do this, and in fact, significant statements to this effect have been broadly reported.

It is not sufficient, however, to look backward. It appears to me more productive to attempt to move ahead with today's growing appreciation of the importance of research and to deepen and intensify this by considering its basis in the central truths of the faith, particularly as these have been illumined by the emphasis of Vatican II.

RESEARCH AS PARTICIPATION IN THE MYSTERIES OF FAITH

The Trinity and Creation

Going back again to the Council of Nicaea, we see that by stating the consubstantiality of the Son with the Father, it clarified more than the mode of the relationship of research to the life of the Church. By declaring that the Word, who proceeds from the Father, is no less than the infinite Truth that is God himself, it identified the real foundation for scholarship and the basis for hope for its success. The fact that all has been created through the Word implies a basic homology between the universe and the Divine Word. If, then, in creation the human intellect is divided from the world and the mind distinct from the body, the Christian knows that they are not alien. Neither he nor his universe is merely opaque. Rather, to the full extent of their reality both are intelligible and open to successful investigation by the mind. In this light, research can be seen to play a unique healing function in a divided world.

A related factor and one greatly stressed in Vatican II is that of participation, through which each created reality reflects the power of God's creative life. This theme of participation has rich implications. It extends beyond the relation of bishops to the pope, and includes all members of the Church. That each person (and each social unit) reflects in his actions the creative activity of the Creator evokes on the part of each an attitude of activity and responsibility. No university, no researcher is simply an agent of a bishop, any more than any bishop is simply an agent of the pope. Each has his identity and each is called upon to exercise it creatively and in his own right.

The Incarnation

Basically we must remember that the incarnation shows the way in which this activity of man is incorporated into the work of Christ. His Body is continued in those who have been incorporated into him by baptism. His members share in his mission.[9]

All things—matter and spirit, creation and Creator—are united in Christ as the supreme affirmation of reality. This presents the basic relatedness of the many branches of knowledge from physics through theology. Each science studies intensively a dimension of nature or of man and, as it develops, progressively reflects an aspect of God's creative action. In various interdisciplinary combinations, as with philosophy and theology, they can reflect the transforming character of the Incarnation. Step by step—in a progressive and often elusive manner—through the joint resolution of particular problems a clarification of the image of Christ can gradually take place.

Redemption

Christ has come also as Redeemer. To a world which sin has often deformed, Christ comes as healing light. To scholars whose work has been impeded by divisions between Churches, by rivalries between institutions, and by alienation between and within professional groups, Christ comes as reconciling truth. To researchers whose efforts have been marred by purposes too isolated or selfish, Christ comes as a light that is life. Despite the many factors which divide and obscure, the message of redemption and reconciliation provides grounds for hope that research can lead to understanding and that this can unite and heal.

Redemption, achieved once and for all in the Paschal mystery, must be renewed and implemented throughout history. In our vocation, the development of interdisciplinary and interuniversity research capabilities is an important contribution to the realization of redemption and reconciliation in the world today.

A RESEARCH AGENDA

Given these ample implications for research, the Second Vatican Council, through its document on The Church in the Modern World

[9]John 1:4–9.

164

(*Gaudium et Spes*), drafted the agenda for a massive and continuing program of research. It requires the highest capabilities of the human mind because it would search out the profound mystery of God himself. It involves all of man's arts and sciences for it concerns the understanding and realization of the divine purpose in all things. It should be a creative response to the full range of human needs, because it should be part of the continually unfolding pattern of God's creative power at work.

The needs of the Church for research are multiple and far reaching. Indeed, they can never be stated once and for all, for they evolve with the flow of history. Statements of specific research needs, therefore, are indicative rather than exhaustive. I cite only by way of example certain issues on which research is needed, to illustrate both the extent of the research needed and the breadth of the implied invitation to all parts of the scholarly community.

The Nature of the Church

Just as the providential development of understanding made it possible for the Church, at the time of Nicaea, to ask new questions and thereby grow in its understanding of the mystery of the Trinity, it is possible and even necessary today to face new questions which arise concerning the nature of the Church and its sacramental life. For example, the Church has long been called—and is—the Body of Christ. This was also beautifully expressed in scripture in terms of the vine and its branches. But the Church has been called—and is—society as well. The evolution of social theory thus raises new questions and opens new possibilities for articulating the meaning of the initial scriptural metaphors.

Social theory has evolved through systems analysis and other theoretical modes. These make it possible increasingly to restate the metaphors in which the nature of the Church was first expressed. Indeed, it would seem essential to do so, for social upheavals of recent years indicate that people increasingly understand their life in society in new and, as yet, unassimilated manners. If the Church is to be able to give its answer in faith to the questions of Christian self-identity troubling her members, a cooperative research effort will be needed.

Finally, as the Church is a sacrament and her sacraments are signs, it becomes important to draw upon contemporary theories of hermeneutics in order to understand and express in more contemporary terms, her nature, her sacramental life and the way this can be shared by her members. Again, as in the days of Nicaea, this does not imply substituting philosophy for faith. It is the necessary condition, however, for finding the response in faith to the questions that face the Church at this stage of our cultural development. Without such answers, the Christian's understanding of his life in Christ can hardly avoid being restricted to the ongoing level of social awareness, with its merely human norms and limitations.

The Mission of the Church

In carrying out its internal mission to its members other examples come to mind. In developmental psychology, understanding the levels of cognitive growth and the development of the child's capacity for moral judgments are important. Both have immediate and important implications for learning theory and for the mission of the Church to teach the Good News. To identify these implications for moral education, family life, and sacramental practice requires combinations of research capabilities from, e.g., psychology, education, and religious studies. The intent of such work certainly would not be to substitute a particular ethical or psychological theory for the gospel message. It should contribute, however, to understanding better the way in which a child who is baptized in Christ can grow in his awareness of the implications of his new Life.

Combinations of theologians, sociologists, lawyers, and economists are needed to identify the conditions of the modern family, as well, and to determine which factors promote and which destroy the life which the Church communicates.

Christian Witness in the World

The mission of the Church, however, goes far beyond the life of those who, by baptism, have been incorporated into Christ. It extends to witnessing to the world the transforming message of the one who came to redeem all men. The Church is called to witness the meaning of Christ's salvific sacrifice throughout the entire catalogue of issues, ranging from the beginnings and dignity of human life, through man's use of his resources and his ability to share these equitably for the needs of all, to the excruciating questions of death for/or in peace with one's fellow men and with God. As St. Augustine well understood when he wrote his *City of God*, the answers to these questions, though given in principle, must be worked out in the ongoing historical process. Research, by means of increasingly sophisticated scientific methods, must investigate, analyze and interpret this reality. Indeed, the major constitutive element in any cultural stage is precisely this analysis and interpretation which we call research.

It is upon this understanding, moreover, that the future is built. If we are called to the loving contemplation of truth itself, the present mode of this vocation is to transform our fractured world in order to restore, in the words of Pope John XXIII, the visage of Christ in all things. This can be done only by research that is adequate for achieving a real understanding of the present situation and comparing it to the Christian ideal. The purpose of such a comparison cannot be to condemn the present or to construct fictitious utopias. Rather, the purpose of research must be to gain direction, to determine the limitations which circumstances impose upon the range of available options, to select what is truly desirable, and to work effectively and progressively toward that goal.

STRUCTURES FOR RESEARCH

The Universities

In this work one of the calculations to be made concerns the availability of resources. Perhaps the most central factor in such a calculation is the research capability of the Catholic universities. Certainly it would be quite unrealistic to think of these universities carrying out all the work that is needed by themselves. In fact, effective research can be carried out only within the national and international professional community. It would be unrealistic, however, to believe that the interpretation of the past and present, or the discernment of future options needed for a Christian understanding will arise by accident from some sort of general research pool. No large organization in the world today subsists on the hope that others will do for it the work required in order to understand its own distinctive identity. Certainly, the Church cannot do so. That is why we turn to you.

Your deliberations face a range of options. At one extreme is that of leaving professors and graduate students in isolation to make uncoordinated decisions concerning their research projects. Other options provide some degree of coordination of their work and of the supporting work of other scholars. Progress must lie in this latter course.

What is required of the individual researcher is simply, but essentially, that in the midst of the welter of concerns which flow from his instructional mandate, he give due importance to the research needs which he can assist. I agree that the selection of topics for research should be made by the individual faculty member himself. However, he needs to make these decisions with awareness of the true nature of research and the extent to which people depend upon his research for the quality of their life.

The task of the university—your task—is to determine what is desirable and feasible within the area of research. What type of resources are needed? What is available in personnel and equipment? How can they be brought together? It is your task to determine what structure will make it possible to work on these questions with the continuity needed, and what will bring research to fruition and provide for its communication to other scholars and to the university's various constituencies.

The NCCB/USCC

As General Secretary of the NCCB/USCC, I can say that the Conferences' needs for research are great indeed. Above, I mentioned that these fell on three levels; here, I would like to speak in operational terms.

The Conference is essentially a coordinating unit of the episcopacy and of many areas of the life of the Church, from education to ecumenical affairs; from justice and peace to minority concerns; from ministry to liturgy and all avenues of pastoral concern. It is the task of the conference staff to explore policy options and make recommendations, to assist in drafting statements and pastoral letters, and to represent the Church to the government and other bodies regarding issues which notably affect, not only the life of the Church members, but the lives of all men in this nation and in the world. It is neither possible nor desirable for the small staff of the Conference to attempt to carry out the intensive research required for this work. The mission of Christ will not be adequately served unless some way is developed for the Conference to draw upon the scholarly community with its diverse and expert capabilities for the research needed.

Recently, the Catholic learned societies in this country have formed a

Joint Committee. Among other purposes this committee has the task of responding in some degree to the research needs of the Conference. This initiative has been greatly appreciated and concrete planning is already underway for a meeting in June which will assist an ad hoc committee of the Conference preparing a document on moral values.

The NCCB, for its part, has designated Archbishop Quinn as its liaison with the scholarly community. It will add to its staff a scholar whose task it will be to follow the state of various issues as these arise in the work of NCCB/USCC, to formulate the related research questions and to communicate these to the scholarly community as an invitation for its contribution. Conversely, this scholar will be charged with bringing to the attention of the appropriate unit in NCCB/USCC issues and information which the scholarly community wishes to suggest to the NCCB for attention in its policy making function.

This scholar's work can be fruitful only to the degree that you provide a point of contact which has the needed information and structure. As with the learned societies themselves, the nature and purpose of any such structure must be determined by you in terms of your goals and purposes. I would request, however, that among these you include a research contribution to the work of the NCCB/USCC.

It is needed. It is requested. And it will be welcomed.

Appendix 1:

Participants in the Symposium

BISHOPS

Most Rev. Joseph L. Bernardin, D.D., Archbishop of Cincinnati, President, National Conference of Catholic Bishops

Most Rev. William D. Borders, D.D., Archbishop of Baltimore

Most Rev. Edwin B. Broderick, D.D., Bishop of Albany

Most Rev. Joseph R. Crowley, D.D., Auxiliary Bishop, Fort Wayne-South Bend

Most Rev. John S. Cummins, D.D., Auxiliary Bishop of Sacramento

Most Rev. Carroll T. Dozier, D.D., Bishop of Memphis

Most Rev. Raymond J. Gallagher, D.D., Bishop of Lafayette

Most Rev. Mark J. Hurley, D.D., Bishop of Santa Rosa

Most Rev. Bernard F. Law, D.D., Bishop of Springfield-Cape Girardeau

Most Rev. Raymond W. Lessard, D.D., Bishop of Savannah

Most Rev. William E. McManus, D.D., Auxiliary Bishop of Chicago, Chairman, Education Committee, United States Catholic Conference

Most Rev. Cletus F. O'Donnell, D.D., Bishop of Madison, President, National Catholic Educational Association

Most Rev. James S. Rausch, D.D., General Secretary, United States Catholic Conference

Most Rev. John J. Sullivan, D.D., Bishop of Grand Island

Most Rev. Edmund C. Szoka, J.C.L., Bishop of Gaylord

MAJOR SUPERIORS

Sister Melissa Waters, O.P., Education Committee, Leadership Conference of Women Religious

Sister Barbara Thomas, S.C.N., President, Leadership Conference of Women Religious

Rev. James L. Connor, S.J., President, Jesuit Conference

Brother Thomas More Page, C.F.X., Executive Director, Conference of Major Superiors of Men

Rev. James E. Gallagher, C.S.C., Assistant Provincial, Congregation of Holy Cross

UNIVERSITY AND COLLEGE ADMINISTRATORS

Rev. Theodore M. Hesburgh, C.S.C., President, University of Notre Dame

Rev. Hervé Carrier, S.J., President, International Federation of Catholic Universities and Rector, Gregorian University, Rome

Rev. Donald P. Merrifield, S.J., President. Loyola-Marymount University, Los Angeles

Sister Joan Bland, S.N.D., Vice President, Trinity College, Washington, D.C.

Rev. John P. Richardson, C.M., Executive Vice President, De Paul University, Chicago

Sister Irenaeus Chekouras, R.S.M., President, St. Xavier College, Chicago

Sister Candida Lund, O.P., President, Rosary College, River Forest

Dr. John M. Duggan, President, St. Mary's College, Notre Dame

Sister Jeanne Knoerle, S.P., President, St. Mary-of-the-Woods College, Indiana

Msgr. Francis P. Friedl, President, Loras College, Dubuque, Iowa

Sister Kathleen Feeley, S.N.D., President, College of Notre Dame, Baltimore

Rev. John W. Padberg, S.J., President, Weston School of Theology, Cambridge

Rev. Ernest J. Bartell, C.S.C., President, Stonehill College, North Easton, Mass.

Sister Mary Agnes Mansour, R.S.M., President, Mercy College, Detroit

Dr. Norbert J. Hruby, President, Aquinas College, Grand Rapids

Rev. Michael Blecker, O.S.B., President, St. John's University, Collegeville

Sister Alberta Huber, C.S.J., President College of St. Catherine, St. Paul

Sister Joyce Rowland, O.S.F., President, College of St. Teresa, Winona

Rev. Thomas M. O'Donnell, Academic Dean, Carroll College, Helena

Brother Patrick S. McGarry, F.S.C., Executive Vice President and Provost, Manhattan College, Riverdale

Sister Dorothy Ann Kelly, O.S.U., President, College of New Rochelle

Brother John G. Driscoll, C.F.C.,
President, Iona College, New
Rochelle

Rev. Kenneth F. Slattery, C.M.,
President, Niagara University, New York

Rev. Joseph B. Dorsey, C.S.B.,
Acting Dean, St. John Fisher
College, Rochester

Dr. Robert E. Wolverton, President, College of Mount St.
Joseph, Ohio

Rev. Raymond A. Roesch, S.M.,
President, University of Dayton, Ohio

Brother Daniel Burke, F.S.C.,
President, La Salle College,
Philadelphia

Rev. William Bryon, S.J., President, University of Scranton

Rev. Charles D. Sherrer, C.S.C.,
President, King's College,
Wilkes-Barre, Pennsylvania

Sister Lucille McKillop, R.S.M.,
President, Salve Regina
College, Newport, R.I.

Brother Stephen V. Walsh,
C.S.C., President, St. Edward's University, Austin

Rev. William J. Sullivan, S.J.,
Provost and Acting President, Seattle University,
Washington

SCHOLARS/ SPECIALISTS

Dr. Frank Broderick, Department
of History, University of
Massachusetts

Rev. David Burrell, C.S.C.,
Chairman, Department of
Theology, University of
Notre Dame

Sister Anne Carr, Assistant Dean,
The Divinity School, University of Notre Dame

Mr. Richard W. Conklin, Director, Department of Information Services, University of
Notre Dame

Msgr. Lawrence Corcoran, Director, National Catholic
Charities, Washington, D.C.

Rev. James A. Coriden, Dean,
Washington Theological Coalition, D.C.

Rev. Clyde F. Crews, Bellarmine
College, Louisville

Mr. Joseph Cunneen, Editor,
Cross Currents

Sister Agnes Cunningham,
S.T.D., St. Mary of the Lake
Seminary, Mundelein

Dr. Charles Dechert, Department
of Politics, Catholic University of America

Dr. Michael Donnellan, Siena
Heights College, Adrian;
Representative, College
Theology Society

Msgr. John J. Egan, Director,
Center for Pastoral and
Urban Ministry, University
of Notre Dame

Dr. Joseph F. Fahey, Director,
Peace Studies Institute, Manhattan College, and General
Secretary, Pax Christi,
U.S.A.

Dr. Donald A. Gallagher, Vice President, De Rance, Incorporated, Milwaukee

Dr. Michael V. Gannon, Department of History, University of Florida, Gainesville

Sister Ann Ida Gannon, Chairperson, Commission on Colleges and Universities, North Central Association

Rev. Edward Glynn, S.J., Woodstock Theological Center, D.C.

Msgr. John R. Gorman, Ph.D., Pastor, St. Michael's Church, Orland Park, Illinois

Msgr. Joseph Gremillion, Fellow, Center for the Study of Man, University of Notre Dame

Dr. Margaret Healy, Department of Philosophy and Academic Dean, Rosemont College

Rev. J. Bryan Hehir, Associate Secretary, Department of Social Development and Peace, United States Catholic Conference

Rev. Donald E. Heintschel, Chairman, Association of Learned Societies and Scholars, Toledo

Rev. Eugene F. Hemrick, Coordinator-Elect, Research and Policy Development, Department of Education, United States Catholic Conference

Dr. Raymond Herbenick, Department of Philosophy, University of Dayton, Ohio

Sister Carol Frances Jegen, Director, Graduate Program, Religious Studies, Mundelein College

Mr. Harry G. John, President De Rance, Incorporated, Milwaukee

Sister Franzita Kane, C.S.C., Professor Emeritus of English, St. Mary's College, Notre Dame

Rev. Eugene Kennedy, Department of Psychology, Loyola University, Chicago

Sister Karen Kennelly, C.S.J., Dean, College of St. Catherine, St. Paul

Msgr. Francis J. Lally, Secretary, Department of Social Development and Peace, United States Catholic Conference

Rev. Philip Land, S.J., Visiting Associate, Center of Concern, Washington, D.C.

Rev. Robert Monticello, Associate General Secretary, United States Catholic Conference

Dr. John D. Mulhern, Associate Dean, Professional Studies, State University College at Buffalo, N.Y.

Rev. Philip Murnion, Office of Pastoral Research, Archdiocese of New York

Msgr. John F. Murphy, Executive Secretary, College and University Department, National Catholic Educational Association

Dr. Ralph M. McInerny, Department of Philosophy, University of Notre Dame

Rev. George F. McLean, O.M.I., Department of Philosophy, Catholic University

Dr. John T. Noonan, Professor of Law, University of California, Berkeley

Dr. Robert B. Nordberg, Dean, School of Education, Marquette University

Dr. Michael Novak, Editor, EMPAC

Dr. David O'Brien, Department of History, College of the Holy Cross, Worcester

Msgr. Wilfrid H. Paradis, Project Director, Research, Policy and Program Development, United States Catholic Conference

Brother Leo V. Ryan, C.S.V., Dean, College of Business Administration, University of Notre Dame

Mr. Russell B. Shaw, Secretary for Public Affairs, United States Catholic Conference

Mr. Donald Thorman, Publisher, *National Catholic Reporter*

Rev. David Tracy, The Divinity School, University of Chicago

Dr. A. Peter Walshe, Department of Government and International Studies, University of Notre Dame

Dr. Evelyn Eaton Whitehead, Department of Theology, Director of Field Education, University of Notre Dame

Dr. Gordon C. Zahn, Department of Sociology, University of Massachusetts

PLANNING COMMITTEE

Rev. Ernest Bartell, C.S.C., President, Stonehill College

Rev. David Burrell, C.S.C., Chairman, Department of Theology, University of Notre Dame

Rev. James A. Coriden, Dean, Washington Theological Coalition

Msgr. John J. Egan, Director, Center for Pastoral and Urban Ministry, University of Notre Dame

Rev. Bryan Hehir, Associate Secretary, Department of Social Development and Peace, United States Catholic Conference

Sister Franzita Kane, C.S.C., Emeritus Professor of English, St. Mary's College, Notre Dame, Indiana

Msgr. John F. Murphy, Executive Secretary, College and University Department, National Catholic Educational Association

Dr. Michael Novak, Bayville, New York

Dr. David O'Brien, Department
of History, College of Holy
Cross

Dr. Evelyn Eaton Whitehead,
Field Education, Department
of Theology, University of
Notre Dame

Sister Karen Kennelly, C.S.J.,
Dean, College of St.
Catherine, St. Paul

Rev. George F. McLean, O.M.I.,
Secretary, Inter-University
Committee on Research and
Policy Studies, Catholic
University

Brother Leo V. Ryan, C.S.V.,
Dean, College of Business
Administration, University
of Notre Dame

Most Rev. Joseph Crowley, D.D.,
Auxiliary Bishop, Fort
Wayne-South Bend

Most Rev. Raymond J. Gallagher,
D.D., Bishop of Lafayette,
Indiana

Most Rev. Bernard F. Law, D.D.,
Bishop of Springfield-Cape
Girardeau

Most Rev. Edmund C. Szoka,
J.C.L., Bishop of Gaylord,
Michigan

Rev. William M. Lewers, C.S.C.,
Provincial, Congregation of
Holy Cross

Brother Thomas More Page,
C.F.X., Executive Director,
Conference of Major
Superiors of Men

Appendix 2:
Research Needs

During the last year information which could be analyzed in terms of research needs has been gathered in the consultations for the Bicentennial, for the pastoral on moral values and for the Catechetical Directory. The following specific calls for research have come from the IFCU and from the NCCB/USCC.

The International Federation of Catholic Universities, at its General Assembly in Delhi during August, 1975, established a Coordinating Center for Interdisciplinary Research and in its various resolutions emphasized the need for interdisciplinary research on

a. Contemporary problems regarding the relation of the realm of intellect and faith, especially those issues amenable to interdisciplinary inquiry where the various sciences and the doctrinal, moral or institutional interests of religion may be involved;

b. issues and research areas reflecting a concern for the integration of knowledge;

c. pressing human problems, especially those reflecting common concerns of diverse parts of the world or ecumenical concerns and opportunities; and

d. issues regarding population, including the relations between personal and national development and the manner of exercising responsible parenthood.

Dr. Charles Dechert, Professor of Politics of The Catholic University of America, has been asked to organize the first stages of this initiative.

NCCB/USCC senior staff officers were asked by the Inter-University Committee on Research and Policy Studies (ICR) and The Joint Committee of Catholic Learned Societies and Scholars (CLS) to identify what they conceived to be the principal doctrinal, moral and social issues confronting the contemporary Church and amenable to clarification by focused research inquiry. The recognized issues tended to coalesce in the following three areas: the church: its structures, ministries and sacraments; Christian life and the family; and the church in the contemporary world.

A. The Church: Its Structures, Ministries and Sacraments

1. To examine in greater theological, philosophical and sociological depth the nature and structure of the Church as the Mystical Body of Christ, as Sacrament, as organization, as social system, etc.

2. a. To define more closely and to justify the various activities undertaken by the Church (directly and indirectly) and the relative levels of effort assigned to them; and

b. more specifically, to define the properly sacramental and religious ministries of priests, deacons and other institutional roles in Church and their relations one to another.

3. In terms of A 2 b above

a. to define more accurately the knowledge, personal attributes and skills needed in the various religious ministries; and

b. to apply this to structuring the curriculum and the personal formation of the clergy, in and out of the seminary.

4. a. To study in greater detail the rewards and dissatisfactions attendant on religious ministries and their relations to personality structures, with particular regard to the reasons for leaving priestly ministry;

b. to study the careers of laicized priests with special consideration to the possible religious functions they may serve; and

c. to examine the functions, satisfactions and frustrations of permanent deacons, and the effect of their ministry on their marriages and vice versa.

5. To examine in greater detail the state of scholarly debate on the following issues, with an objective statement of divergent and alternative positions:

a. foundational theology (apologetics);

b. the sacrament of Confirmation;

c. the indissolubility of marriage;

d. the theology of the single life;

e. the role of women in the Church, including the question of ordained ministry; and

f. intercommunion.

B. Christian Life and the Family

1. To study the condition of modern family life, specifically regarding:

    a. what personal and social factors tend to preserve or to destroy the family unit;

    b. the relation between the family unit and the development of the moral standards and comportment of its members;

    c. the problem of the divorced Catholic in its personal, moral and religious dimensions.

2. To study:

    a. the practice and incidence of abortion in relation to diverse legal policies; and

    b. the interaction and the long range physical, psychological, social and religious effects of abortion/abortion procedure on women and on their future children.

3. To investigate the cognitive and emotional growth of the child as related to:

    a. moral and religious development;

    b. the relation of family values to outside values training;

    c. the impact of the media on the family;

    d. the effect of violence and secularist values in TV programming and advertising;

    e. the possible and probable effects on the family of video discs and other developing communications technologies.

4. To explore:

    a. activities directed at the evangelization of youth by the major faiths;

    b. the role of schools in promoting vocations;

    c. practical programs of youth ministry; and

    d. the preparation of adults for reception into the Church.

5. To study:

    a. why the private religious school option was chosen;

    b. the religious attitudes, values, habits of Catholic students in Catholic and public high schools and colleges;

    c. the impact of religious schools, with specific attention to disadvantaged, poor or linguistically/culturally different children; and

    d. trends in religious education regarding attendance, effectiveness and alternatives.

6. to examine:

a. the content and quality of released time denominational education of students in public schools;

b. its impact on students and on school administrators;

c. the role of the public school in teaching values, theoretically and practically, especially values relating to money, family, education, sexuality, marriage, employment, drugs and alcohol; and

d. the teaching about religion in public schools, its content, quality and impact.

C. The Church in the Contemporary World

1. To explore:

a. the characteristics of an adequate moral or ethical methodology and the Roman Catholic contribution thereto;

b. the relation of morality and law in a pluralistic society;

c. the extent to which a religion, in terms of its values and commitment, can/should influence business, government, education; and

d. the obligations which arise from the Vatican II declaration on religious liberty.

2. To examine the role of the mass media in shaping the knowledge, perceptions, attitudes, values and beliefs of the Catholic community, in particular:

a. the way its impact differs in function of age, sex, education, culture and lay, religious or clerical status;

b. the gaps in knowledge in the communications literature relating to the Catholic community; and

c. ways in which the media may be accessed and employed in the interests of religion (including evangelization), of the Catholic community, and of Christian culture and moral values.

3. To examine:

a. the implicit or explicit images of the person characteristic of modern society and their moral and social consequences;

b. ways of shaping institutions to human nature and human scale; and

c. questions regarding quality of life and the "correct" relation of man to nature.

4. Because Christian witness to the world requires accurate understanding of the present situation and its comparison to the Christian ideal, to explore:

a. this ideal in terms of a range of more or less desirable/acceptable social institutions and arrangements;

b. the direction(s) which should be pursued on the basis of a Christian or Catholic consensus; and

c. the range of realistic options given the actual historical situation.

5. To determine:

a. on which public issues the American Church should express policy recommendations to the Congressional and Executive branches of the U.S. government;

b. to what extent these should express a consensus in the American Catholic community—and what level of consensus;

c. the extent to which a consensus should be expressed officially (NCCB/USCC), and/or unofficially through organs of American Catholic opinion; and

d. whether a Catholic position should be sought and expressed on:

    (1) national health insurance
    (2) health care (costs, education, services)
    (3) housing and community development
    (4) human rights (race, ethnicity, sex, age)
    (5) full employment, income maintenance
    (6) economic recovery
    (7) domestic food production and distribution
    (8) reform of prisons and correctional institutions
    (9) land use
    (10) energy policy
    (11) handgun control
    (12) rural life (preservation and protection of family farms)

(Many of these issues revolve around questions of distributive justice and the use of public as opposed to non-public approaches to the allocation of scarce resources.)

6. To explore the spectrum of views and the degree to which it is prudent and desirable to express official Catholic views on such issues as:

a. the preservation of the defective, the expiring and the severely traumatized;

b. the limits of personal and group freedom;

c. a social pluralism permitting life styles contrary to the Christian conscience, especially when these are expressed publicly and/or may prove inviting to the immature;

    d. the nature of a "normal" personality, a "healthy" group;

    e. motivation and behavior as a function of culture; and

    f. character development and socialization processes in an essentially secular culture.

    7. To study issues relating to the interrelations between the "free exercise" and the "establishment" clauses in the first amendment to the U.S. Constitution.

    8. To research policies and practices which might provide guidance in Church relations with government, other churches, *et al.*, and the degree to which these may or should be developed, directed and implemented in a centralized fashion.

Bibliography

Papal Documents:

"The Mission of a Catholic University," (May 13, 1972), *The Pope Speaks*, 17 (1972), 131–140.

"New Tasks for Catholic Universities," (Nov. 1972) *The Pope Speaks*, 17 (1972), 355–357.

"Research as a Form of Charity," Address to Pontifical Academy of Sciences. *L'Osservatore Romano*, weekly English Edition, May 8, 1975, p. 2.

"Address to the Rectors of Jesuit Universities," *L'Osservatore Romano*, weekly English Edition, August 21, 1975, pp. 3, 8.

* * *

The Catholic University in the Modern World. Document of the Second Congress of Delegates of Catholic Universities of the World, Rome, 1972. (Available at College and University Department, NCEA, $1.00.)

———. Same Document, with Commentary by Richard W. Conklin. *Notre Dame Journal of Education*, Vol. 4 (Fall 1973), pp. 197–216.

The Spiritual Function of the Catholic University and its Function as Critic. Report of the X General Assembly of the International Federation of Catholic Universities, Salamanca, 1973. (Available at Secretariat Permanent, F.I.C.U., 77 bis, rue de Grenelle, 75007, Paris).

Carrier, Hervé, S.J., President of F.I.C.U. and Rector, Gregorian University, Rome, "Does the Church Really Need Catholic Universities?" Address at Annual Meeting, College and University Department, NCEA. (Available, C & U Dept., NCEA. $1.00.) See also *Origins*, Vol. 2, p. 733.

Crosson, Frederick, and James Hitchcock, "How is the College or University Catholic in Practice," Delta Epsilon Sigma Lectures, annual meeting of College and University Dept., NCEA, 1975. (Available at C & U Dept., NCEA. No Charge.)

McLean, George F., O.M.I., ed. *Inter-University Cooperation in Research*. The Concorde Publishing Company, Lancaster, Pa., 1975.

Orsy, Ladislaus, S.J. "Interaction Between Church and State," *Catholic Mind*, Vol. 73 (February 1975), pp. 38–57. (Valuable Detailed Notes and Biblio.) (Available also at C & U Dept., NCEA. No Charge.)

Rausch, Very Rev. James S., General Secretary, United States Catholic Conference, "The Importance of Research in the Church," *Origins*, 5, pp. 28–29.

For additional publications in *Origins* which treat the nature of Catholic Colleges and Universities and the relationship between the academic community and the magisterium, see *Origins*, 5, marginal notations, pp. 28–29. Listed there is also the bibliographical information regarding the address by Archbishop Joseph Bernardin, ''What Can the Church Expect from the Catholic Universities,'' which was distributed with the first announcement of the Evangelization Symposium, July 1, 1975.

Occasional Papers. Publications of C & U Dept., NCEA. First issue contains addresses of Archbishops Bernardin and Baum, Father Madden, S.J., and a series of research reports by Rev. Andrew Greeley on Catholics as scholars. Second issue focuses on undergraduate theology at Catholic Institutions. (Both available at C & U Dept., NCEA. $1.00 per copy. Rates for quantities.)